LORETTO

LORETTO

THE SISTERS AND THEIR SANTA FE CHAPEL

MARY J. STRAW COOK

Museum of New Mexico Press
Santa Fe

FOR THE SISTERS OF LORETTO

Frontis: Altar of the Chapel of Our Lady of Light, ca. 1965. LMA.

Loretto: The Sisters and Their Santa Fe Chapel, Revised Edition, was originally published in 1984 under the same title in a clothbound edition.

Project editor: Mary Wachs
Design and Production: Bruce Taylor Hamilton
Composition: The text is set in Centaur; Display typography in Albertus Light.
Manufactured in China
10 9 8 7 6 5 4 3 2

Library of Congress Cataloging-in-Publication Data

Museum of New Mexico Press
Post Office Box 2087
Santa Fe, New Mexico 87504

Abbreviations in the captions refer to the following collections:

CSF	College of Santa Fe, St. Michael's High School Archives	LMA	Loretto Motherhouse Archives
MNM	Museum of New Mexico Photo Archives	NMSA	New Mexico State Archives, E. Boyd Collection

CONTENTS

*Santa Fe, New Mexico, April 1881. View to the east with Chapel of Our Lady of Light, "La Casa Americana" (convent)
to the right, and unfinished Academy building to the left. At the extreme left, the unfinished St. Francis Cathedral.
Photo by Ben Wittick, MNM 15820.*

FOREWORD

Of all the historical wonders for which New Mexico's venerable capital of Santa Fe is renowned, the Miracle Staircase in the beautiful little Gothic Revival Loretto Chapel has to rank among the most spectacular. The tight spiral of stairs, offering no visible means of support, seems to defy both gravity and the basic rules of structural engineering. Yet, there it is, more than a century old, uncoiling upward to the choir loft, a work of high craftsmanship and beauty that each year thrills thousands of visitors.

Constructed in the last quarter of the nineteenth century, Our Lady of Light Chapel (now called Loretto Chapel) was located on the campus of the Loretto Academy for Girls, astride the old Santa Fe Trail. The school finally closed its doors in 1968, to be replaced by the Inn at Loretto hotel complex. Today, the chapel is the only remaining building left from the original academy, which had been conducted by the Sisters of Loretto.

In 1984 Mary J. Straw Cook, a lifelong Santa Fe resident and dedicated musician and historian, published the first edition of her *Loretto: The Sisters and Their Santa Fe Chapel*. It represented a landmark effort to document the history and architecture of the structure, to identify the actual builder of the staircase, and to describe the chapel's remarkable Debain harmonium. The volume included a rich collection of historical photographs.

Very quickly the attractive book went out of print and for many years has been unavailable, although much coveted by collectors. Fortunately, the author has undertaken a second edition, with revisions scattered throughout and a staircase chapter that has been entirely reworked to produce a new solution to the builder mystery.

Almost by accident, the author stumbled upon the name of a French immigrant and artisan, François-Jean Rochas, who it now appears was responsible for the construction of the famed stairway. By combing archives, including the Loretto Motherhouse Archives in Nerinx, Kentucky, and through research trips to France, Mary J. Straw Cook has been able to build a strong case in support of Rochas as the key figure in the story.

Strangely, Rochas had long been known to historians and popular writers, but in another context. Right after Christmas 1894 he was found shot to death at his small ranch in Dog Canyon, east of the Tularosa Basin in southern New Mexico. The murderer was never apprehended.

The late C. L. Sonnichsen, in his popular book *Tularosa, Last of the Frontier West*, incorporated a chapter on Rochas and described events leading up to his slaying. But he failed to mention his carpenter skills or to link him in any way with the Loretto staircase, although he noted that Rochas knew and liked Archbishop Jean-Baptiste Lamy of Santa Fe. Discovery of the Frenchman's earlier career and contribution in the New Mexican capital would be left to the author of the present volume.

I am indeed pleased that the author has asked me to prepare this brief foreword to the new edition of her book. For a fact, I can state that she is a capable and tenacious researcher who over the years has uncovered significant bodies of information on New Mexico history, relating to subjects overlooked by professional scholars. Her *Loretto*, while primarily a labor of love, is nevertheless a significant addition to the religious history of the American Southwest. I applaud its republication and commend the book to the attention of all those with a serious interest in our regional culture.

MARC SIMMONS

PREFACE

NEW MEXICO would have no reservoir of nineteenth-century women's history today were it not for the Sisters of Loretto. These courageous women left the green, rolling hills near Bardstown, Kentucky, made famous by composer Stephen Collins Foster in his nostalgic ballad "Old Kentucky Home" for the frontier. The sisters traveled to the rugged West in 1852 with Bishop Jean-Baptiste Lamy and endured countless hardships to bring religion and education to an area filled with outlaws, fur-trappers, trail merchants, and everyday people. Had the sisters read one particular history of New Mexico of unknown source, they might not have come. It said that Santa Fe "bears an evil reputation as one of the most reckless and miserable towns on the globe."

In 1993 after traveling to Nerinx, Kentucky, the writer became keenly aware that few New Mexicans knew the quantity of New Mexico women's history deposited in the Loretto Motherhouse Archives. The Motherhouse is a large farm nestled among the distilleries of the Kentucky bourbon country. With the generous cooperation of the Sisters of Loretto, twenty-eight microfilm reels of Loretto's New Mexico history were photographed and deposited in the New Mexico State Archives in Santa Fe.

Since the first edition of this book in 1984, unforeseen historical information has come to light, including the name of the Frenchman who is believed to have been the carpenter of the spiral staircase in Loretto Chapel. Also, the approximate location of the burial site of Loretto Sister Alphonsa Thompson, who died en route to Santa Fe in 1867, has been established along the Santa Fe Trail in Kansas.

The author has made many trips to Auvergne and Isère, France, to continue the research on the French architects and workmen who came to Santa Fe during the nineteenth century. Some of the buildings bearing the architectural stamp of their heritage no longer stand.

To the Sisters of Loretto, who have shown limitless patience regarding my queries about their history, I am unendingly grateful, particularly the late Sister Florence Wolff, Loretto Motherhouse archivist. To Peter Eidenbach of Human Systems Research, Inc., Tularosa, New Mexico; Peter Greene of the New Mexico State Park and Recreation Division, Department of Natural Resources, Santa Fe; and Marie-Françoise Bois-Delatte of Grenoble and Vif, France, I owe much for the sharing of their research and knowledge on François-Jean Rochas accomplished during the establishment of the Oliver Lee Memorial State Park in 1978. Through the courtesy of Marie-Françoise Bois-Delatte, I met the surviving relatives of Rochas, Mme. Davagnier and Mme. Terrier. Rochas, before immigrating to America, had been an attendant at the wedding of their grandfather. My thanks to Yves Armand, president of the historical society in Vif, and to Marc Maire, a member of La Fédération Compagnonnique, a centuries-old French artisans' guild, of Echirolles, France.

It is my great fortune to have made so many French friends and to have met scholars who assisted me during the course of the Loretto Chapel research: Daniel Patoux, Valbelle, Ardèche; Stefáne Gomis, Clermont-Ferrand, and Marie-Claude Boismenu, Volvic, in Puy-de-Dôme; and Dr. Jean-Pierre Marliac, Paris, and Michel Allaeys, Croissy-sur-Seine, both of Aigueperse, Puy-de-Dôme. Twentieth-century Santa Feans are indeed indebted to Noël Grenet of Cusset, Allier, for our first glimpse of chapel architect Projectus Mouly. And always, my thanks to the many families for the photographs of their artisan-ancestors, a contribution of enormous importance to this book. Jane and Larry Monier (grandson of Quintus), Tucson, Arizona, assisted in the significant discovery of the Monier letters and biographical data both in the U.S. and in France.

Special acknowledgment goes to the Archbishop of the Archdiocese of Santa Fe (owner), who has generously permitted the Debain harmonium to remain in Loretto Chapel to be played and heard as it was in the 1880s by the Sisters of Loretto. I wish to acknowledge the scholarly analysis of the Debain mechanism and registration by Dr. James M. Bratton of Denver, Colorado. He also carried metal reeds from London to the U.S. to replace missing ones in the Debain harmonium.

The support, friendship, and abiding faith of the Kirkpatrick family, owners of Loretto Chapel, encourage my research endeavors on the Sisters of Loretto and their magnificent chapel.

Altar and nave of Chapel of Our Lady of Light, ca. 1895. LMA.

LIST OF ILLUSTRATIONS

CHRONOLOGY

1812   Friends of Mary at the Foot of the Cross (Sisters of Loretto) founded by Father Charles Nerinckx in Kentucky as one of the first American communities of sisters dedicated to teaching.

1850   Pius IX creates the Vicariate Apostolic of New Mexico and names Jean-Baptiste Lamy as its first vicar apostolic.

1851   Vicar Apostolic Jean-Baptiste Lamy arrives in Santa Fe.

1852   Lamy brings the first Sisters of Loretto to New Mexico with Mother Magdalen Hayden as their first superior.

1853   Sisters open the Academy of Our Lady of Light in Santa Fe. Vicariate of New Mexico elevated to a full bishopric and named the Diocese of Santa Fe.

1855   Sisters open their novitiate.

1857   Sisters purchase property on which the Chapel of Our Lady of Light is built.

1873   Construction of chapel begins.

1874   First stones cut for chapel.

1875   Diocese of Santa Fe elevated to an archdiocese, and Lamy becomes its first archbishop.

1878   Chapel of Our Lady of Light completed and blessed on April 25 by Vicar-General Peter Eguillon. First funeral held in chapel upon the death of Loretto Sister Bridget Armijo.

1880	Construction of academy building begins.
	Construction of spiral staircase begins.
1881	Completion of spiral staircase.
	Completion of academy building.
1884	Bishop Jean-Baptiste Salpointe receives the Pallium in chapel and becomes the second Archbishop of Santa Fe.
1885	Statue of the Sacred Heart of Jesus blessed by Archbishop Lamy.
1887	Chapel consecrated by Archbishop Lamy.
	Handrailing of spiral staircase added.
1888	Sisters construct new convent on site of Casa Americana.
	Archbishop Lamy dies.
1893	Property line in front of chapel straightened and low stone wall built shortly thereafter.
1896	Via Crucis canonically erected in chapel and Stations of the Cross (tin) changed to begin at the Epistle instead of Gospel side.
	Sisters close novitiate.
1898	Electricity installed in chapel.
1901	Chapel receives second and present roof of pressed terneplate.
1902	Sisters donate land beside the Santa Fe River to City of Santa Fe for Sparks Avenue, presently called Alameda.
	Auditorium to east of academy constructed.
1908	First renovation of chapel occurs: first heat (steam) added, second floor (hardwood) laid, round window above altar and windows in sanctuary opened.
	Present confessional and altar railing installed.
1910	Present Gothic altar installed.
	Present Stations of the Cross erected.
1920	Construction of Albertina Hall begins.
1927	Second renovation of chapel occurs; interior fresco paint of walls and apse.

1928	Construction of Miguel Chávez Building begins.
1939	Conversion of stable and chicken houses into St. Francis Opportunity School.
	Spiral staircase first appears in Robert Ripley's "Believe It or Not" column.
1946	Colonnade designed by John Gaw Meem constructed connecting side doors of chapel to convent.
1950	Third renovation of chapel occurs: exterior cleaned and reconditioned, storm windows added to protect stained glass, interior cleaned and painted (frescoes freshened), linoleum tile laid over hardwood floor, brass light fixtures installed, pews revarnished, and spiral staircase reinforced and repaired.
1957	Spiral staircase appears for second time in Robert Ripley's "Believe It or Not" column.
1968	Academy of Our Lady of Light (Loretto) closes.
1970	Oscar E. Hadwiger of Pueblo, Colo., claims his grandfather, Yohon L. Hadwiger of Vienna, Austria, built spiral staircase in chapel.
	Chapel historically plaqued by the Historic Santa Fe Foundation.
1971	Sisters of Loretto sell 4.5 acres of property, including the chapel, to the Inn at Loretto.
	Demolition of old Loretto buildings begins, and abandoned convent catches on fire.
1972	Conservation of chapel interior and exterior begins: new hardwood floor laid (third) and spiral staircase raised and stabilized, exterior gable finials and iron cross copied and replaced, tin roof and Our Lady of Lourdes statue painted, and colonnade to convent removed.
1973–75	Construction of the Inn at Loretto.
1982	Second colonnade constructed connecting side doors of chapel to the Inn at Loretto, stabilizing temperature and climate of chapel interior.
	Original Alexandre-François Debain harmonium (ca. 1867) conserved

and returned to chapel choir loft by the Historic Santa Fe Foundation and Archdiocese of Santa Fe.

Princess Anne, daughter of Queen Elizabeth of Great Britain, visits chapel.

1993   Our Lady of Lourdes statue lowered to ground level from rooftop to stabilize the base of statue.

1996   The Inn at Loretto sold to Noble House.

Chapel ownership retained by the Kirkpatrick family, original owners of the Inn at Loretto.

François-Jean Rochas named by author as builder of spiral staircase.

Hardwood floor in chapel replaced (fourth).

CHAPTER 1

THE SISTERS
OF LORETTO
AND HOW THEY GREW

Them nuns do a heap sight of good in this god-forsaken country.
Kit Carson

To MOTHER MAGDALEN HAYDEN and the Sisters of Loretto, the dedication of their beautiful stone chapel in Santa Fe on April 25, 1878, brought to a rapturous conclusion twenty-five long years of hoping, dreaming, and working. Designed and built by talented Frenchmen, Italians, Germans, and New Mexicans, it was something to be proud of, and the citizens had watched it rise from the earth with special interest. The *Santa Fe New Mexican*, published in both Spanish and English and variously named *Daily*, *Weekly*, and *Santa Fe New Mexican*, had reported in 1875:

> It was begun somewhat more than a year ago and, since then, work has been continuous by a small force of engineers so that now the rear and sides have attained their full height. In fact, we observe that the first stones for the vaulted roof have been set.
>
> The size of the chapel is 25 feet in width by 75 feet in length including the sanctuary in the middle and the sacristy behind it. It is built in the

Gothic style. It is constructed entirely of cut stone using a light brownish sandstone from the Archbishop's quarry east of the city. It has beautifully sculpted pillars and ornaments at the door and windows within; two alcoves for statues are also surrounded with artistically embellished sculpted designs while the walls are substantially supported by strong buttresses. All these comprise a substantial degree of perfection, with artistic design as well, which is not exceeded, if equalled, west of the Mississippi valley.

The ceiling is going to be of stone from a porous lava formation which, with its characteristic lightness, permits this type of roofing and thereby renders the entire structure not only strong in the extreme but absolutely fireproof. The stained glass windows, which were made to order in France with equalled depictions, have already arrived and are ready to be installed when the work is sufficiently advanced.

The chapel was designed by Mr. Mouly, the architect in charge of the Cathedral, who is of quite high standing and of good taste and judgment as an artist. The erection of this beautiful and substantial edifice, such an asset to the territory, is entirely due to the effort and thought that Archbishop Lamy has given to the work. It will not be completed for another year. When finished it will be one of the permanent ornaments of the ancient city and a monument of great credit to the enterprise of its planner.[1]

"The design of the front and especially of the massive doorway, 18 feet high, is superb. The most of the stone is cut and carved in readiness to be placed. . . ." reported an October 1876 *Daily New Mexican* account.[2] In June 1877 the same newspaper stated that "work is steadily going on at the new Catholic chapel in the convent grounds, the ornate front now occupies the special attention of the builders."[3] Evoking criticism from almost every corner, the seventy-one-foot-tall stone building and spire, so visible from all directions in a city built on the "squatted plan," became fair game for architectural kibitzing.[4]

From a distance, just now, as with a late style of bonnet, it is somewhat difficult to tell which is the rear and front end of the new Convent Chapel. The front of the building is not yet finished, but the rear end is surrounded by a neat little cupolo [sic] or belfry shingled with slate, which makes that end appear as the front. However, we suppose the architect knows his business.[5]

Finishing touches on the Chapel of Our Lady of Light became apparent in November 1877.

Workmen are putting in the stained glass in the high, gothic windows, and soon, we imagine, that "dim religious light" so characteristic of the interior of these gothic-built style of churches, will add a certain sanctity to the service.[6]

On April 25, 1878, the sixty-sixth anniversary of the founding of their society, the Sisters of Loretto celebrated the blessing of the Chapel of Our Lady of Light.

The chapel was blessed by Father Vicar Eguillon [vicar-general to Lamy] assisted by six clergymen, viz. Rev. Father Truchard, Courbon, Seux, Valezy, Remuzon and Mariller. Father Vicar celebrated the mass and preached, the Sisters sang and the Brothers' band played at intervals. After mass, the clergymen, Mr. P. Mouly, the architect, and the workmen who had built the chapel repaired to the repast prepared for them. An entertainment was then given them by the pupils.[7]

The dedication of that stone chapel, still a New Mexico landmark, was interesting in and for itself, but its implications were far-reaching—for the town, for the Territory, and for the Church. It symbolized the arrival of education and a special kind of culture to a region which had desperately needed both. It brought a

Santa Fe, ca. 1882, looking north down Old Santa Fe Trail. Loretto Chapel can be seen at upper right-hand side of image. Photo by William Henry Jackson, CSF.

Bishop Jean-Baptiste Lamy, ca. 1860s. MNM 35878.

group of dedicated women for special service in an area still remote. It gave the Catholic Church a new weapon in its fight against ignorance and sin. It showed New Mexico and the world that the Sisters of Loretto and the things they stood for were there to stay.

When the advance guard of the sisters arrived in 1852, they came as missionaries, sent out from their home convent in Kentucky to serve the western frontier. If not the first order of sisters asked by Bishop Lamy to cross the plains in wagons on the Santa Fe Trail, the disciplined Sisters of Loretto ultimately proved to be the most tenaciously qualified for the impending rigors. In 1812 Father Charles Nerinckx, a native of Belgium who had fled the French Revolution, founded the Friends of Mary at the Foot of the Cross in Kentucky as one of the first American communities of sisters dedicated to teaching.[8] However, their first rule made no explicit mention of teaching non-English-speaking children, but Lamy encouraged them to do so.[9] Bishop Lamy explained:

> Spanish and music would be indispensable. The Spanish language is easy . . . . Santa Fe having a population of about six thousand people, all Catholic except for four hundred Americans would very easily support a school, besides there is no doubt they would receive boarders from all parts of the territory.[10]

The voice crying in the wilderness summoning them to distant New Mexico belonged to the pioneer Bishop Jean-Baptiste Lamy, Father Latour in Willa Cather's novel *Death Comes for the Archbishop*, a major figure in southwestern history, who arrived in 1851. His career began inauspiciously when he found that he would have to clear his status with the bishop in Durango before his charges and his priests would accept him. Mexican Bishop José Antonio Laureano López de Zubiría, claiming no knowledge of Rome's mandate of a newly established vicariate encompassing the Rocky Mountains, grudgingly ceded power to its new bishop. Rome had sent a Frenchman who spoke Spanish but argued in Latin. The reluctant ces-

Reenactment of the 1867 burial on the Santa Fe Trail of Loretto Sister Mary Alphonsa Thompson. Photo taken in 1902. MNM 67741.

sion had meant 3,000 miles in the saddle for Lamy, the traveling bishop who crossed the United States twelve times.[11] The Bishop of Agathonica, *in partibus infidelium,* once said he lived off the fat of the land as he traveled about his diocese astride his bay mule—*El Bendito Frijole y El Santo Atole*—the blessed bean and the holy corn mush.[12]

After a three-month absence to establish his authority, Lamy returned in January 1852 to Santa Fe, seat of his bishopric, where his church was already foundering with priestly distrust. Culture was pitted against culture. The basis of the conflict was that of frontier Catholicism as developed by the Spaniards in direct opposition to the French Catholicism of Bishop Lamy, an unyielding prelate. A well-documented confrontation between the educated Padre José Martínez of Taos and his bishop spanned sixteen years. The debate lingers even today.[13]

The battlefront loomed everywhere in a vicariate apostolic larger than Lamy's native France—rebellious priests, crumbling church buildings, lack of money, illiteracy of much of the population, and predatory Indians. Perhaps the greatest discomfort to a Frenchman was the isolation from accustomed amenities. Bishop Lamy wrote that Santa Fe churches reminded him of "the stable of Bethlehem."[14] It was an earthy description of their mud walls with straw binding whose ceilings were of the same material layered over adzed *tablas*, *latillas*, and beams. But a cathedral of adobe? Not for an Auvergnat and his stone-chiseled Romanesque heritage.[15]

Santa Fe's new Vicar Apostolic Lamy, *l'étranger*, proved himself no stranger to the organization of priorities. He wrote for sisters to teach, priests to pray, and money to build new churches; his pleas covered two continents in four languages. Again, in April 1852, Lamy rode off to gather up Sisters of Loretto from Kentucky, priests from Lyon, and money from Paris; France had long been the nursery and treasury for American missionaries. From the distant Vatican, Jean-Baptiste Lamy needed a sustained dialogue of understanding and cooperation, spoken in both Italian and Latin. Bishop Lamy always needed travel expense money in any language.

"I would pay their expenses for coming to this place," Lamy wrote in September 1851 from Santa Fe to Bishop John Baptist Purcell (later archbishop) of Cincinnati, Ohio, place of Lamy's consecration in a cathedral known as "the bishop factory."[16] Lamy continued:

> The Sisters of Notre Dame will receive a letter from me . . . . I have asked
> them if they could send me a few Sisters to establish a good school . . .
> or if it was not in their power to spare any Sisters, will you please write
> to Emmitsburgh to obtain three or four Sisters of Charity . . . or Sisters
> of any order.[17]

Appointed to the foreign mission called Santa Fe were Loretto Sisters Matilda Mills, superior, Catherine Mahoney, Magdalen Hayden, Rosanna Dant, Monica Bailey, and Roberta Brown. Only four of the original six ever reached the City of

Holy Faith, a place Indians called "Dancing Ground of the Sun." Mother Matilda Mills died of cholera on board the steamer *Kansas* between St. Louis and Independence, Missouri, nineteen days out of Bardstown, Kentucky, point of departure that June 27, 1852.[18]

Independence, a restless breeding ground of trail-pilgrims and their diseases, became the western rendezvous for both the Santa Fe and Oregon Trails in 1831. By 1852 Westport had replaced Independence as the main outfitting center for westward wagons. Westport, now called Kansas City, was ten miles farther west near the good landing at Kansas. Thus they avoided the treacherous fording of the Big Blue River of the Missouri.[19]

The morning of July 17, 1852, Mother Matilda's cortège, led by the vicar apostolic of New Mexico, climbed the long hill from Todd's warehouse near Blue Mills landing on the Missouri River six miles from town. Stopped once by a sheriff to forbid entrance into Independence (river towns enforced quarantines on cholera victims), the procession reached the pasture of a Christopher Stayton, east of Courthouse Square.[20]

Sisters Magdalen Hayden and Monica Bailey also contracted the deadly cholera. Both survived in a tent sweltering with July heat. Too weak to continue the journey, Sister Monica turned back to Kentucky at Independence after recuperating but arrived in Santa Fe three years later with the second contingent of Loretto Sisters.[21] Magdalen Hayden became the new superior of her flock and continued the difficult journey. The 780-mile trip was described in her practice Spanish letterbook.

> On the 1st of August, the train began to travel, but they had scarcely gone a few miles, when one of the wagons broke down. In the evening, on account of the rain, the Sisters' tent could not be pitched, and they remained in the carriages. During the night, the rain continued to pour, accompanied by high wind, thunder and lightning, which terrific storm made their frail tenement sway to and fro and creak as if ready to fall to pieces. . . . The next Sunday, mass was said in Pawnee Fork, where they

spent the whole day and killed the first buffalo. From that time on, immense herds of these wild animals were more frequently met with. . . . After two or three days, they reached Ft. Atkinson at a short distance from which they had the greatest panic yet experienced on their route, they saw themselves surrounded by three or four hundred Indians the greater part of the day. The intention of these savages was not known, these were their hunting grounds, but the caravan deemed it safer to travel all night, as Indians do not attack travelers by night. They crossed the Arkansas and reached Cimarron the following Sunday 12th of September; they there halted two days in order to rest the jaded animals that had been crossing the sandy plains. On the 14th or 15th near the Colorado River, they met the Vicar General, Father J. P. Machebeuf, with a party of men and animals that had come to meet His Lordship. The Friday following they arrived at Ft. Bartly [Barclay] where they slept under roof for the first time during nearly two months.[22]

After a short rest at the bishop's ranch, seventeen miles to the south, the Sisters of Loretto arrived in Santa Fe dusty but triumphant. Mother Magdalen recalled that the sisters arrived in late afternoon. Boisterous crowds of men, women, children, dogs, and burros filled the narrow, crooked streets making it almost impossible for the carriages to pass under triumphal arches of "beautifully-colored silks, gold crosses, artificial flowers, and mirrors" erected by the friendly townspeople.[23] Church bells pealed as they rode to the old *parroquia*, where priests escorted them to a front row of seats in a hitherto seatless church. A welcoming *Te Deum* was sung to the accompaniment of violins and guitars.[24] The arrival of travelers offered a form of entertainment which Santa Feans welcomed in a town of few diversions.[25] On a moment's notice, and usually signaled by lookouts posted on Talaya Hill, Santa Fe laid down its pen and plow to greet the wagon trains of arrivals who had camped outside of town in order to spruce up their appearance.[26]

Three months almost to the day had elapsed since the four sisters first began their journey aboard the *Lady Franklin* to St. Louis up the Mississippi River from Louisville.[27] Mother Magdalen found herself frustrated on arrival. She wrote:

> Although the Sisters had at length reached their journey's end, after a long and perilous journey, they could not open school not knowing the Spanish language; they therefore, began to study it, the Bishop himself having given the first lessons while yet on the steamboat. They also received instructions in the language from a secular teacher, and the Bishop had two Mexican girls brought to the house, Margarita and Francisquita Sandoval.[28]

The first Sisters of Charity, who arrived in 1865, had been housed and fed by the Sisters of Loretto. In her 1877 memoirs an empathic Sister of Charity, Blandina Segale, found other reasons for dismay, writing:

> Imagine the surprise of persons coming from places where houses are built with every convenience and sanitary devices, suddenly to find themselves introduced into several oblong walls of adobes, looking like piled brick ready to burn, to enter which, instead of stepping up, you step down onto a mud floor; rafters supporting roof made of trunks of trees, the roof itself of earth which they were told had to be carefully attended, else the rain could pour in; door openings covered with blankets; the while giving you a prison feeling; a few chairs, manmade and painted red; a large quantity of wool which they were assured was clean and for their use; no stoves, square openings in corners where fires could be built—all those things were to constitute their future home. Where the bare necessities of life were to come from was an enigma to them. Strangers to the country, the customs, and the language, do you wonder that a lonesome feeling as of lingering death came over them? Can you doubt that it would have required the presence of an angel to convince

them that the preparations made for them were princely? Yes, so they were, for the time and country. This had been the Bishop's Palace, which he was giving up, so that the Sisters might have easy access to the Cathedral![29]

These four pioneer Sisters of Loretto constituted the first organized women's community in New Mexico. Moreover, the Academy of Our Lady of Light, opened in Santa Fe by them in 1853, was the first permanent school for girls in the territory. The sisters' carefully recorded student account and cash books, kept in Spanish until 1875, read like a roll call of dominant historic New Mexico families of their time—Sena, Cháves, Castillo, Perea, Tully, Beaubien, Bent, Leroux, Spiegelberg, Spitz, Delgado, Ortiz, St. Vrain, Connelly, Otero, Armijo, Maxwell, Montoya, Abréu, Pendaries, Wallace, Manderfield, Staab, Luna, Huning, and Giddings. An uncle of the Bent sisters, Teresina and Estafina, made the comment, "Them nuns do a heap sight of good in this god-forsaken country."[30] His name was Kit Carson. The Sisters of Loretto mingled with the famous people of the era, often sharing the bustling marketplace on the Plaza at the foot of the Santa Fe Trail, which was only a block from their convent and school. The history recorded by the sisters during their one-hundred-and-sixteen-year tenure comprises the greatest single source available of New Mexico women's history.

Mother Magdalen Hayden wasted no time in setting up her books. A $74 notation, dated the day of her arrival in Santa Fe, entered the first cash-on-hand. It is followed by contributions over the ensuing year of $72.35 from various sources and $508 from *"El Señor Obispo."* Expenditures totaled $359.62, and of that $222 were repaid to the bishop. Income generated by student tuition needed to be supplemented. The sisters sold fruit and vegetables from their garden, entered into *partidos* with Pablo and Roman Moya, and taught Mrs. Willi Spiegelberg French lessons.[31] Listed as *gastos* (expenditures) in the sisters' books, purchases were regularly made in the fine Spiegelberg Brothers' store on the Plaza.

In January 1853 the Academy of Our Lady of Light opened with ten boarders and three day-scholars. In six months the boarders totaled twenty and the day-scholars twenty-two.[32] "The establishment for the education of Misses is located in the most beautiful part of the city," the sisters advertised in the local newspaper. They described the building loaned to them by Bishop Lamy as "commodious and surrounded by a large garden which affords ample room for the scholars to take exercise in." Subjects taught included orthography (spelling), reading, writing, grammar, arithmetic, geography, history, and for the more advanced, astronomy with use of the globe, natural history, and botany. Social refinements for young ladies such as needlework, drawing, painting, music on the piano and guitar, vocal music, and French, all were taught in a discipline that was, according to the sisters, "mild and parental, and at the same time strict and positive." English and Spanish were taught and spoken equally.[33] Mother Magdalen told of her students:

> In the people, and especially in the girls, whom we have under our care, I find the girls docile and easy to govern. Generally speaking, I think they have more talent for imitation than for the hard study of the sciences. They have a strong predilection for music.[34]

"The sisters called me rebukingly, albeit lovingly, 'their little heretic'," Marian Russell wrote in her charming memoirs entitled *Land of Enchantment*. Marian, a student under the sisters in Santa Fe in 1854, rationalized her non-Catholic background: "After all, what does it matter what we believe so long as we live charitably by the Golden Rule, help to feed the hungry and clothe the naked?" She continued:

> I have never forgotten how the sisters tried to instill into our hearts a little bit of culture, and the hard time they had so doing. They planned our lessons so that we might learn poise and self reliance along with readin', writin' and 'rithmetic. Textbooks were sometimes laid aside and our lessons went on with marvelous ease and quietness. Each day we

were supposed to do something for others, to help others. It was there that I learned how much easier it is to act than to think. Contemplation defied me. Unholy thoughts came pressing up, not to be denied at the hour of contemplation. Shape after shape, grotesque and ugly, forced themselves into my child's mind. If you think contemplation is easy, just try it.[35]

Initially, the sisters shared an adobe house and courtyard with Bishop Lamy near the parroquia; the house, furniture, and land were his. The summer of 1853 brought many sorely needed repairs to this house, and for lack of space, Lamy moved to another house. A devastating rainy season in 1854 tested the sisters' patience and mud roof. Mother Magdalen recalled:

We have been moving our things and especially our beds from place to place in order to find a dry spot in which to put them. . . . This is the greatest discomfort of the Mexican houses, because otherwise they are very comfortable, being cool in summer and warm in winter.[36]

Then came a smallpox and cholera epidemic. Mother Magdalen seemed shocked at herself as she wrote:

Last winter every one in the house was vaccinated except her whom they thought too old to ever take smallpox. But I'm telling you that they were all very wrong. Sunday, three weeks ago, on reaching the convent after High Mass, Sister Catherine [Mahoney] and I stopped to look at one of the day students whose face was red and pock-marked. It was a novelty to us because it was the first time we had seen any one who had that disease and we feared nothing. But the following week she took sick with a violent fever and soon the pox was discovered. . . . The people here do not seem to fear this disease but you know what horror they have of it in the United States of America. The poor Sisters who are coming will be much terrified to hear that we had had this sickness in the house.[37]

Yet another insidious disease, tuberculosis, habitually took lives in religious communities in great numbers. Its communicability went unrecognized, and the Convent of Our Lady of Light beside the Rio Santa Fe was no exception.[38] The sisters perpetually boiled the well water to avoid a typhoid-fever outbreak among the students. One of the students, Eva Hilton of Socorro, New Mexico, sister of the future hotel-magnate Conrad Hilton, exhibited symptoms erroneously thought to be typhoid. Born in New Mexico and a student under the sisters at Mount Carmel School in Socorro, Conrad Hilton befriended the Sisters of Loretto throughout his lifetime.[39]

The academy in Santa Fe flourished beyond all Catholic expectations in spite of epidemics. Within one year, thirty boarders and thirty day-scholars greatly outnumbered the four sisters. The bishop made arrangements to bring more sisters on his return from Rome in January 1854, but his logistics went awry.

On account of no clear understanding between the Bishop and the Loretto Superiors with regard to defraying traveling expenses, the Sisters did not meet him in St. Louis; he therefore continued his journey to Westport where he waited for them more than a month, using the provisions intended for the journey. Finally not hearing from them, he started with his company on the first days of Oct. and reached Santa Fe on the 19th of November.[40]

Four more sisters arrived in 1855, and life in the already cramped quarters reached an impasse. Again, Bishop Lamy relinquished his recently acquired residence to the sisters, eventually selling it to them in 1857 for $3,000 though he had paid $4,000 for it. The debt was to be paid in three payments of $1,000 without interest. The ever-frugal sisters liquidated the debt in one year.[41] Lamy also conveyed all the furnishings of the large house to them, including fifty bedsteads, piano, chairs, carpets "and a thousand other useful and valuable things, without mentioning what he gave to the chapel."[42] The Casa Americana with its surrounding orchard and garden, originally built as a hotel, was conveyed in an instrument dated February 3, 1859, designating:[43]

> a certain parcel of land and house situate in the City of Santa Fe bounded and described as follows—bounded on the south by the Rio de Santa Fe, on the West by a street leading from the southeast corner of the public plaza of the said city of Santa Fe to the town of San Miguel, on the north by a house and lands the property of Alexander M. Jackson and lands late of Damaso Lopez and on the east by the street which passes from the Parish church to the Rio de Santa Fe. . . .[44]

Named La Casa Americana by the local population, the pitched, shingle-roofed house of two stories represented an architectural style brought to Santa Fe by the nineteenth-century Americans. Today, however, flat-roofed pueblo-style buildings remain the hallmark of much of Santa Fe's historic core. To the sisters from Kentucky, Casa Americana possessed a comfortable familiarity and furnished them a much larger chapel measuring seventy-four by twenty-four feet with only a partition separating it from the school.[45]

Between 1857 and 1863 seven pieces of property were acquired to establish the large and well-protected Loretto site on which the Chapel of Our Lady of Light and the Inn at Loretto rest today. Mother Magdalen wrote of her constant anxiety about money and property:

> I believe I told you we had bought another piece of ground which we had rented since we came to this house, in order to hang out the clothes, and for other uses. This land cost us $1,000. Half of this sum is now paid and

Path to the Sisters' graveyard, ca. 1885. East wall of Convent grounds to left. LMA.

we have until next September 1, 1860 to pay. A few years ago I thought we could not continue here through lack of resources. At that time I was wont to say: "Oh, if the house were only ours, perhaps we could support ourselves." Now not only the house is ours, but we have besides five new rooms, with the house and land already mentioned and which is more we have some novices and postulants who are so well educated that no community can desire better.[46]

In May of 1863 Mother Magdalen wrote, "We now own the entire block so that there will always be a street between us and our nearest neighbors."[47]

CHAPTER 2

TIMES
of TROUBLE,
TIMES of JOY

Poor New Mexico! So far from Heaven, so close to Texas!
Governor Manuel Armijo, Department of New Mexico

FROM THE SECOND-STORY WINDOW of the sisters' convent, one could view the end of the Santa Fe Trail and the multitudes who reached it—traders, immigrants, curious travelers, and soldiers. In the early 1860s, there were Confederate soldiers. In 1862 the Civil War thundered up the Rio Grande Valley from El Paso. Confederate Brigadier General Henry H. Sibley planned to capture New Mexico with his Texas Mounted Volunteers (the Confederate Army of New Mexico) but suffered unexpected defeat at Glorieta, eighteen miles southeast of Santa Fe. His supply lines severed, Sibley and his starving Texans straggled into town, though the majority escaped through Albuquerque. Mother Magdalen described the events preceding the battle:

How much terrible destruction has been wrought by this Civil War during the past months in our once happy and peaceful nation! Even our poor and distant Territory has not been spared. The Texans without pro-

19

Left to right: Loretto academy, chapel, and La Casa Americana, ca. 1890. Photo by D. B. Chase, Southwest Museum, 20652

vocation have sacked and almost ruined the richest portions and have
forced the most respectable families to flee from their homes, not pre-
cisely by bad treatment, but by obliging them to deliver to them huge
sums of money. . . .[1]

All military and civil officials had abandoned Santa Fe to reach Fort Union,
hoping to gather military strength to stop the advance of the Texans. Before leaving, the Union soldiers set fire to the provisions left behind. Mother Magdalen
wrote:

> On purpose or by accident, two houses, which had served as quarters for
> the soldiers where there was a considerable quantity of flour were set on
> fire on the same day which fanned the flames of those burning houses.
> The terror which I felt is inexpressible, because of the danger to our
> house and what increased my fear was to see stacks of hay in the govern-
> ment corral not very far from the fire. . . .[2]

The Texans marched from Santa Fe toward Fort Union on March 25, 1862, and
encountered Union forces in Apache Canyon. A second skirmish resulted in a
Confederate defeat, and the Texas Volunteers returned to Santa Fe. Mother Magdalen recalled that fearful time:

> Saturday, March 29, 1862, the enemy retired to Santa Fe. They began to
> arrive here in the afternoon in parties of different numbers and they
> continued entering until almost noon on Sunday. We could hear them
> passing all night, our convent being on the street through which they
> had to pass, but we did not know to which side they belonged until
> morning when we saw by their clothes that they were Texans. Some
> came on horseback, others on foot, and others were almost dragged to
> the city. All were in a most needy and destitute condition in regard to
> the commonest necessities of life.

LORETTO

The 30th of March, 1862, was the day on which I was most frightened. The whole city was in the possession of the Texans, who had placed their cannons in a defensive position so as to prevent the entrance of those from the north. On that day the wind was furious, the Bishop was not here and I did not know what to do because I feared they were going to have a battle here and that our house would be burned or thrown down by the cannon balls. But, thank God, nothing happened to us.

The Texans had their quarters all around us. Some of them climbed on the roof of the day school and one entered the school itself through a window which looks out over the street, asking if the room was unoccupied. He opened another window which opens on the courtyard but as soon as he saw some Sisters he went out through the street window. When they climbed on the roof and when this man entered the school, I sent for the Bishop and he notified the commander and so they ceased to molest us.

We did not have school for the day students for three weeks because there were so many Texans passing and repassing through the streets. Many times I thought what a blessing of God it was that they had finished our wall last year. Otherwise, these Texans would have been able to enter and to look through our windows whenever they took the notion to do so. It seems that our Lord had foreseen what was for our good. . . .

The whole time the Texans remained here we were in continual distress of mind. We hid many of our provisions for fear they would pay us a visit when they found no more in other places. . . .

I don't believe I would ever have known how to appreciate the blessing of peace had I not experienced the effects of war.[3]

A Lt. Alfred B. Peticolas was one of the Texas Confederates camped near Mother Magdalen's convent. This is what he wrote in his journal about Santa Fe:

Santa Fe, ca. 1890. Looking north on Old Santa Fe Trail, the Santa Fe River in foreground, convent buildings to right, "La Casa Americana," Chapel of Our Lady of Light, and Academy tower showing just over chapel roof. CSF.

24

Like all Catholic towns, this one abounds in bells and it is not very harmonious to hear them all chiming for matins, and vespers mornings and evenings, for they do not chord by any means, but the noise is rather disagreeable than otherwise, but there is nothing more inspiring than to hear one of these bells "sprinkling with holy sounds in the air," their deep solemn tones ringing through the valley in which the town is situated. They bring recollections thronging to my mind, memories of the long-gone time when I, a little fellow, clinging to Mother's black-kidded hand and carrying a hymnbook, walked slowly up the carpeted aisle of the old Tab Street Church, Petersburg, Va.[4]

With the disappearance of the Confederates on the long road to Texas, the sisters were no longer in danger of losing life or property, and they were free to carry on the work they had left their far-off Kentucky home to do. Between 1863 and 1869 they opened schools all across New Mexico—at Taos, Mora, Albuquerque, Las Vegas, Las Cruces, Bernalillo, and Socorro. Foundations were established in Colorado and Texas as well. An Act of Incorporation under the laws of New Mexico Territory in 1874 granted the academy status as "a body politic and corporate in law and in fact, by the name, style and title of the Sisters of Loreto [*sic*], and by this name shall have perpetual succession. . . ."[5]

A firm educational foundation thus laid, it was time for the sisters to build the chapel which was the symbol of their mission and the evidence of their success. It rose on the sands of the *ciénega* of the Rio Santa Fe between 1873 and 1878, near the stone Romanesque Revival Cathedral of St. Francis, begun in 1869. Both buildings owed their existence to the zeal and imagination of Bishop Lamy, and their construction went on almost simultaneously. The two buildings shared the same French architects, the same French and Italian stonemasons, the same stone quarries, and the same French priestly supervision.

The cornerstone of St. Francis Cathedral, ceremoniously laid on October 10, 1869, contained among other things gold, silver, and copper coins. A few days later "some heathen with infamous hands" stole the valuables during a "vandalic and

Construction of St. Francis Cathedral around the old parroquia, ca. 1879. LMA.

robber saturnalia" in the city that night.[6] Understandably, any cornerstone cere-
mony for the sisters' new chapel, if ever one was held, intentionally received no
publicity. In their annals the sisters noted only that their new oratory was begun
on July 25, 1873, and the first stones cut on January 19, 1874.

Quarried from the summit of Cerro Colorado near Lamy, sandstone was lowered several hundred feet down a shaft on the north, still visible today, and hauled
to Santa Fe on wagons. A climb up to the quarry reveals an eerie frozen segment
of history. Quarried stones, neatly stacked, await the drop down the shaft as if the
stonemasons had taken a lunch break lasting one hundred years. Porous volcanic
tuft for the ceiling vaults of the chapel came from Cerro Mogino, twelve miles
west of Santa Fe. Arroyo Saiz, northeast of town, furnished stone as well.[7]

Architects Antoine and Projectus Mouly were the father and son from Volvic,
France, brought to Santa Fe by Bishop Lamy to rescue the faulty cathedral tower
foundations designed by an earlier but incompetent contractor. Antoine Mouly

returned to France because of blindness, and Projectus continued to direct the chapel and cathedral projects. Progress of the work was threatened when the artistically temperamental Projectus became offended. Charity Sister Blandina Segale wrote:

> Mr. Mouly is the young artist whose nature was so wounded by a person in authority who constantly nagged at him to "work like the other men" that, having warned the inspector, "If your nagging continues, I drop the work"—he did. The work meant the completion of the cathedral and the chapel of the Sisters of Loretto. The unfinished chapel of the Loretto Sisters has been a thorn to me since I came to Santa Fe.[8]

The indomitable, hod-carrying Sister Blandina practiced the sacred art of building schools without the aid of money, known as volunteer labor. Her multifarious adventures included scaling a drainpipe to douse a second-floor fire and the shouldering of the heavy end of a coffin with its occupant to the graveyard, assisted by two volunteer hospital convalescents—a one-legged man with a crutch and a one-armed man as co-pallbearers. A serendipitous acquaintance of outlaw Billy the Kid, Sister of Charity Blandina noted, "Here was a man with qualities to make him great, smothering his best instincts, to become a murderer and an outlaw," taking a professional interest in his case. Administering first-aid for four months to the Kid's partner, shot in the leg and left to die, the sister earned for herself and her habited friends immunity from attack by any of Billy's gang.[9] If time had allowed during the course of Billy's career, she might have had an influence on his life. She claimed to have been instrumental in persuading depressed architect Mouly to continue his work.

> This Mr. Mouly I speak of is the young artist who so interested me while still in Trinidad. All I knew of him was that he was a highly-talented artist and that he had given up the unprecedented honor—for one of his age,

not more than seventeen years, the building of the Cathedral and the Chapel of the Sisters of Loretto, because of his sensitive artistic nature could not brook criticism from one who was not capable of drawing a circle on a square, and yet had the power to "Lord it over him." He withdrew into solitude—that is, from all except one man. Providence gave me the opportunity to discover him.[10]

The one man Sister Blandina referred to was young Mouly's father who had heard via an informant of complaints against his son and urged him to return to France. Projectus refused to leave and wrote his father, "I made no change in your prints nor in the treatment of the workmen, keeping you ever as my master-model." In melodramatic sequence following the chapel completion, the young architect fell into bad company, died of typhoid fever in spite of all the "Charity Girls" (Sisters of Charity) of St. Vincent Hospital could do, and went "to his Judge with a good report" in 1879.[11]

As for the workmen, they were well treated and even ate at the same table with Bishop Lamy. Loretto Sister Margarita Pacheco, Lamy's cook, recalled that she served as many as fifteen workers a day during the chapel construction. Lamy himself served them soup and carved the meat. "Salad was served plain with dill for the French dressing already placed on the table."[12] An August 1879 bookkeeping entry debits $700 paid to Archbishop Lamy "for the board of the men who worked on the new Chapel."[13] The name of A. Rodriguez reoccurs in the 1875–76 cash book as a carpenter working on the "two-story house" or the Casa Americana. Rodriguez, Rafael Martin, both listed as carpenters on the 1870 and 1880 census, and Luis Moya, a stonemason, worked consistently around the convent replacing adobes, shingles, repairing staircases, and general maintenance. Quite likely, these men also worked on the chapel construction. Moya remained for many years as the sisters' loyal maintenance man.

The sisters' books indicate that they made payments to some of the chapel workmen while Bishop Lamy met the weekly or monthly payroll but kept no

Quintus Monier, ca. 1875. The French contractor in the 1880s of St. Francis Cathedral who also worked on the Chapel of Our Lady of Light. Courtesy Michel Allaeys.

books on the construction. Lamy received periodic lump sums from the sisters, which they designated only as "for the new oratorio." Two names appear in an 1881 newspaper ad stating, "Monier & Colloudon [*sic*], contractors, stonecutters & masons" have accomplished much in Santa Fe as "builders of the St. Michael's College and the Sisters' new chapel."[14]

Quintus Monier was the descendant of generations of Monier builders from the village of Aigueperse, France, not far from Volvic. He worked on several Santa Fe residences, the Palace of the Governors, the Federal Building, and St. Francis Cathedral. Remaining in New Mexico until 1896, Monier received a contract to build the Tucson Cathedral in Arizona, where he lived the remainder of his life.[15]

Guillaume Coulloudon had left a wife and three children in Paris, France, to come to America in 1874 to seek his fortune. News of the cathedral and chapel projects and the money to be made was well known in and around Clermont-Ferrand, where Bishop Lamy had attended seminary. Four painful years later, Archbishop Lamy arranged for Coulloudon's family to join him, but his wife no longer recognized her bushy-faced husband.[16]

In Santa Fe known as William, François-Guillaume Coulloudon traveled in this country almost a year before reaching Las Animas and Pueblo, Colorado. There he threw his bug-infested clothing into the Arkansas River, bought new ones, as well as a donkey to carry his pack, and walked the 230 miles to Santa Fe, never returning to France. He wrote to his wife in 1876 that the priests paid well, and how he wished he had arrived sooner because "Pére Mouli" and his son had already stashed away a nest egg of 26,000 francs (approximately $5,000). Much to his surprise after studying English en route, Coulloudon arrived in Santa Fe only to find many speaking French. From Limoges, William Coulloudon described the other three stonecutters as being Auvergnats and "the rest Frenchmen."[17]

Descendants of the Italian stonemasons, who still live in Santa Fe today, document that between 1876 and 1878 Genaro Digneo, his

François-Guillaume Coulloudon, ca. 1890. One of several French artisans who built the Chapel of Our Lady of Light. Courtesy Mariette Coulloudon Cunico.l

brother-in-law, Gaetano Palladino, and Genaro's nephew, Vicente Digneo, were brought to town for the cathedral construction.[18] A reasonable assumption is that these men worked on the chapel as well. By 1880 Carlo and Michelangelo Digneo had arrived, as had Michael Berardinelli. They formed the Digneo-Palladino-Berardinelli construction firm, which built many other significant early New Mexico buildings throughout the state.

Architectural and human problems continued to plague the cathedral and chapel construction beyond 1875, the year Lamy was elevated to archbishop. A further incident hindering construction was the death of the intelligent and qualified French architect Charles François-Philippe Mallet. A man of "very prepossessing appearance," Mallet was shot dead in 1879 by the nephew and namesake of Archbishop Jean-Baptiste Lamy.[19] The affair involving the wife of Jean-Baptiste

Genaro Digneo with his son Ernesto, ca. 1890. One of the Italian workmen who built the Chapel of Our Lady of Light. Courtesy Lydia Valdes Stump.

Lamy, Jr., and Mallet threw the "sleepy-looking—though wide-awake—ancient city of Santa Fe" into "an agitated sea," according to Sister Blandina.[20] After three attempts to render a correctly worded verdict, a jury acquitted J.-B. Lamy, Jr., by reason of insanity.[21] Lamy's marriage to the wealthy Mercedes Cháves, daughter of former Governor José Cháves of Los Padillas, New Mexico, had elevated him from "Foreman of the Gardin [*sic*]" to "Capitalist" between 1870 and 1880.[22] Perhaps his newly acquired high station had some bearing on the outcome of the verdict.

It is worth noting that other rich New Mexico families besides the Cháves clan had much to do with building the chapel. Their wealth was measured in land and in their ubiquitous flocks of sheep. Of the more than $30,000 required to build the Chapel of Our Lady of Light, at a time when a registered letter traveled for ten cents and a load of piñon wood cost thirty cents, the greater part came from three landholding and sheep-raising families: Cháves, Perea, and Montoya. Sister Stanislaus Cháves, sister of doña Mercedes Cháves de Lamy, and also daughter of the union of the powerful Cháves and Armijo families, contributed her estate in her will of 1867.[23] Sister Lucia Perea, born to wealthy Juan Perea and Josefa Cháves of Bernalillo, had donated $25,000 to the Sisters of Loretto by October 1873. Sister Lucia became the first native-born New Mexican superior of the Convent and Academy of Our Lady of Light in 1896. Her wealth, without question, contributed substantially to the chapel construction. The third source was from

Sisters Angela and Rosalia Montoya, daughters of Juan Montoya and Petra Perea, also of Bernalillo. All three families were interrelated. The Loretto annals tell us:

> The building cost about $30,000. The first $6,000 were from Sister Stanislaus' inheritance. Sr. Lucia's money had paid for the property in Las Vegas, $1,500 bought the harp, the mules and carriage, built an addition to the Convent, and supplied the community with clothing for years. Sister Angela and Rosalia's money $18,000 helped to complete [the] chapel and to begin [the] Academy.[24]

Mother Lucia Perea, ca. 1880s. Mother Lucia was the first native-born New Mexican superior of the Academy and Convent of Our Lady of Light. Photo by William Henry Cobb, LMA.

An undated loose sheet of paper tucked in the sisters' cash book headed, "*Debemos por el Nuevo Oratorio,*" listed $6,309 from "Padres Camilo, Fialon, Señors Juan, Miguel, Señor V. Eguillon and Arzobispo." These represented possible loans or donations which contributed to the chapel fund, as did the gold Sister Josefa and Mother Lucia retrieved from Zacatecas, Mexico, where Sister Josefa's father was manager.[25]

Owing its existence thus to many benefactors, the Chapel of Our Lady of Light was at last finished and on April 25, 1878, as already noted, it was dedicated. The venerable Archbishop Lamy missed the chapel blessing because he was traveling in Europe, but the festivities on his return were equal to a second dedication.

Never had he met with so brilliant a reception, triumphal arches, music, speeches, booming of cannon, fireworks, etc. When his carriage passed by the Convent gate, he stopped it, alighted, entered the new chapel, gave his blessing, then proceeded to the cathedral.[26]

Lt. John G. Bourke, an army officer and aide-de-camp in Santa Fe, visited the Chapel of Our Lady of Light not long after its blessing, giving us the earliest known mention of the staircase. On April 18, 1881, he recalled:

Mrs. Woodruff took me with her to see the Convent and chapel of Loretto. We first passed into a large orchard of fruit trees of many varieties, all in full blossom, then across a broad vegetable garden and at last entered the interior corridor of the convent. Faultless neatness was the rule everywhere, not a speck of dirt or dust visible. No one answered our repeated pull on the bell, so we assumed the right to enter the Chapel, the loveliest piece of church architecture in the S. W. country. The nave is an original arch of great beauty, leading to the steps of the main altar in front of which hangs a very large lamp of solid silver. A very well built geometrical stairway leads to the choir where the sisters sing during the celebration of the Holy Offices. It afforded me much pleasure to see this lovely temple, so sweet, so pure and bright, attesting the constant presence and attention of refined and gentle womanhood—far different from the damp dark mouldy recesses of San Francisco, San Miguel or Guadalupe.[27]

The year 1878 saw Sister Bridget Armijo die of consumption, and her corpse was the "first laid out in the new chapel."[28] Archbishop Jean-Baptiste Lamy would also lie in state in the sisters' chapel, encircled by candles which illuminated the worn soles of his well-traveled shoes. Fragile Lamy had presided at the chilly consecration in December 1887, celebrating the debt-free status, customary in the

Catholic Church.[29] Two months later on February 13, 1888, Lamy died. The Father Latour of *Death Comes for the Archbishop* had fulfilled the destiny which entitled Willa Cather's novel. Confessor, banker, confidant, self-appointed chaplain to the Sisters of Loretto, grower of fruit trees, strawberries, and cabbages—this was "the great man whose eagle eye can read one through and through."[30] El Illustrisimo Sr. Arzobispo D. Juan Lamy of Santa Fe died as "Bishop Juan" in New Mexico, and in France, "*Sa mort a ête le fin d'un beau jour*"—his death was the end of a fine day.[31]

Archbishop Lamy did not live to see the total completion of his cathedral, but the Chapel of Our Lady of Light was a reality ten years before his death. The sisters not only had their chapel, but they had it free of debt. Mother Magdalen wrote in 1888 of her relief when this happy condition was attained.

> With regard to temporal affairs, the best and the most consoling (at least for me) information that I can give is that we are, thanks to the dear Sacred Heart, to the Blessed Virgin, and to the Glorious St. Joseph free from debt. Oh! dear Mother you do not know the pangs that I have suffered during so many long years, in consequence of my great and heavy debts, with so very little hope of paying for them . . . .[32]

It had been a long struggle for Mother Magdalen and the sisters. Two major structures had continually drained their resources—the chapel (1873–1878) and the three-story academy building (1880) with mansard roof and tower. These were paid for, but it is worth noting that the sisters continued building and remodeling down through the years. The convent was built in 1892 on the site of the Casa Americana. The auditorium (1902), Albertina Hall (1920), and the Miguel Chávez Building (1928) followed in order—and were paid for. In 1949 the academy building was remodeled to a flat-roofed territorial style.[33]

Santa Fe installed gaslights in 1881 and a city water works in 1892.[34] Heretofore, the sisters had donned bathing gowns, knelt in a tub of solar-heated acequia water from melting snows in the mountains, and washed in two small rooms

Archbishop Jean-Baptiste Lamy lying in state in the chapel, February 14, 1888. Photo by Brother Amian, NMSA.

spanning the ditch and built for that purpose.[35] Not until 1908, when a steam passage was completed from the modern academy building furnace, did the chapel have heat.

Being obliged to heat the chapel which, in the severity of winter could not be used, Sisters Francesca [Lamy] and Lucia [Perea] were sent to Denver (the Archbishop having secured passes on the D. & R. R. [Denver & Rio Grande Railroad] to Española) to examine some establishments heated by steam.[36]

The Loretto annals also state that earlier in 1908 "the old floor was taken up and replaced by hardwood floor."[37] That year brought many more changes.

During this month the Chapel was calzomined. Windows in the sanctuary [were] opened where [the] niches of [the] Blessed Mother and St. Joseph used to be. [The] round window above the altar was opened. An altar rail replaces the old bronze one at which so many holy souls received our Blessed Lord in Holy Communion for fifty years. The altar rail cost was contributed by our pupils. The new confessional was selected by Mother General who had it sent from Louisville.[38]

From 1878 until 1892 the chapel exterior remained much the same, with stone rubble exposed between the Gothic buttresses and a shingled roof. A new metal roof, similar to the one seen today, was added in 1901.[39]

Presiding over Santa Fe atop the chapel roof is the cast-iron statue of Our Lady of Lourdes, hands in praying position. Three meters in height (9.84 feet), the graceful statue was purchased in 1887 from the firm of J. Daniel in Paris, France. The heavy statue was raised to its pinnacle and dedicated on May 19, 1888. During the next fifty years the crescent and halo of Our Lady of Lourdes traditionally illuminated the cool Santa Fe evenings in May and on feast days, after electricity was installed in the chapel in 1898.[40] These lights on the statue have since been removed.

Between 1852 and 1927 the Loretto Sisters opened a total of sixteen schools in New Mexico. One by one, as the state public school system established itself, the sisters reluctantly closed many of their schools. The Academy of Our Lady of Light closed in 1968. Bittersweet moments recall the abandonment of its buildings in the heart of the city and final sale of Loretto's New Mexico roots. The economics of remodeling the convent and academy precluded financial survival for the sisters. The Chapel of Our Lady of Light continues to receive hundreds of thousands of visitors each year.

> Can anyone of the hundreds who admire its beauty today understand what it meant to those nuns to assist at the dedication of that chapel knowing that their faith more than their money went into its erection?[41]
>
> —Mother Magdalen Hayden

Front façade of the Chapel of Our Lady of Light, ca. 1945. LMA. Our Lady of Lourdes presides.

CHAPTER 3

THE CHAPEL
AS ARCHITECTURE

The great point is to put a little reason into what we do,
to proceed as did our predecessors who really did reason . . . .

Eugène Emmanuel Viollet-le-Duc

SAID TO HAVE BEEN PATTERNED AFTER the Sainte-Chapelle in Paris, France, the Chapel of Our Lady of Light is of Gothic Revival architecture.[1] It would be impossible to build the chapel where it stands today because of a historic ordinance enacted in 1957 by the City of Santa Fe. This ordinance prohibits the construction in the historic downtown district of any nonconforming structure, that is, any building which does not adhere to the flat-roofed pueblo or territorial styles of architecture.[2] Yet, it would be difficult to imagine Santa Fe without its Gothic crown jewel, the pitched-roofed, nonconforming Loretto Chapel. Santa Feans are justifiably proud of its beauty and historical significance in their community. Tourists know it by its famous spiral staircase.

Architecture in Santa Fe, New Mexico, has long been an ultra-sensitive subject. One is apt to wonder just how did a chapel designed after the Sainte-Chapelle happen to be built among low-lying adobe walls resembling, according to Englishman George F. Ruxton's 1846 diary, "turf-stacks" in a "prairie-dog town."[3] Even harsher words were written in the early nineteenth century by Josiah Gregg in his well-known *Commerce of the Prairies*. He wrote:

In architecture, the people do not seem to have arrived at any perfection, but rather to have conformed themselves to the clumsy style which prevailed among the aborigines, than to waste their time in studying modern masonry and the use of lime. The materials generally used for building are of the crudest possible description, consisting of unburnt bricks, about eighteen inches long by nine wide and four thick, laid in mortar of mere clay and sand. These bricks are called adobes, and every edifice, from the church to the palacio, is constructed of the same stuff. In fact, I should remark, perhaps, that though all Southern Mexico is celebrated for the magnificence and wealth of its churches, New Mexico deserves equal fame for poverty-stricken and shabby-looking houses of public worship.[4]

The Sisters of Loretto chose Gothic Revival architecture for their new chapel because of the influence of the nineteenth-century Catholic clergy of French origin. Thus we see a New Mexico Gothic Revival adaptation of the Sainte-Chapelle, minus its open porch and lower story (chapels of royal residences in France were two story since the twelfth century, the upper for royalty and the lower for their staff).[5]

Archbishop Lamy held little regard for New Mexico's mud churches with their mud roofs, writing to his French peers that they lacked "architectural character."[6] He often dined with an umbrella over his head to prevent the dust and debris from sifting down onto his favorite supper, oysters.[7] It is quite possible he also delivered his homily in church under an umbrella at various times to protect his fine vestments from a leaky roof. With the arrival of Lamy in 1851 came the first change in the centuries-old building forms and techniques of New Mexico. So to the long list of Lamy changes must be added architecture. Architectural historian Bainbridge Bunting, wrote that Lamy favored "the manner of the Middle Ages" for church architecture.

Rear view of the Chapel of Our Lady of Light, ca. 1945; academy building to the right. LMA.

He and his coworkers, many of whom were also French seem to have included the renovation of church art and architecture along with general ecclesiastical reforms. They appear to have regarded the traditional religious sculpture and painting of the region as uncouth, if not blasphemous, and the simple mud churches as unworthy houses of worship. At the earliest possible opportunity they sought to replace them with buildings and works of art more worthy of the name "Christian."[8]

In 1851 Bishop Lamy wrote that he "would much rather see every church building in New Mexico destroyed than that one finger should be raised against civil authorities."[9] This statement preluded the 1859 trade and destruction of the crumbling Chapel of Our Lady of Light known as La Castrense, built on the Santa Fe Plaza in 1760.[10] By 1866 Lamy's building of eighty-five new churches and chapels, and the repair of the majority of old ones, termed "mutilation by improvement" by author George Kubler, brought about the "Gothizing" of New Mexican churches.[11] Historian John L. Kessell wrote in his monumental *The Missions of New Mexico Since 1776*:

> It is fashionable in our day to berate Lamy and his Frenchmen for their callous disregard of Pueblo and Hispanic culture in general and of indigenous architecture in particular. But conquest is like that. It could hardly have been different, and perhaps worse. What would have resulted, let us imagine, had the Anglo-Irish American hierarchy appointed an O'Shaughnessy to the new see of Santa Fe.[12]

Perhaps if Mother Magdalen Hayden had been more assertive in architectural matters the chapel might have resembled a church in Rath-Clough, Ireland, her place of birth. But the French taste of the thirty-one French priests (out of a total of fifty-one active priests) prevailed. Lamy or his architects surely read the famous French Gothic treatise entitled *Dictionnaire Raisonné de l'architecture française du XI au*

XVI siècle by Viollet-le-Duc, one of the architects who restored the Sainte-Chapelle in 1837 after its secularization during the French Revolution.[13] In his *Entretiens sur l'architecture* (1863–72), Viollet-le-Duc wrote:

> What does matter to us is, that our buildings should be erected in conformity with our customs, our climate, our national genius, and the progress that has been made in science and its practical application . . . . Each building, however little it may differ as regards the programme and means of construction, has a physiognomy peculiar to itself, although we easily recognize by inspecting its general features and its minutest details, that it belongs to such and such a period.[14]

The appearances of New Mexican churches changed rapidly—"for everybody thinks himself something of an architect,—a circumstance which, while it honours architecture, is in some respects detrimental to it. . . ."[15] To their adobe missions, the French resident priests added Gothic touches of belfries and gabled roofs which "made these buildings look more like barns than churches."[16] Father Camille Seux of San Juan, with the aid of his personal funds, built a chapel strikingly resembling the sisters' Chapel of Our Lady of Light in Santa Fe. Father Camille's money had also helped to build their chapel. And, like the Sisters of Loretto, he erected a statue of Our Lady of Lourdes, no doubt ordered at the same time and from the same firm in Paris.[17] Gothic was considered the architecture of Christianity, and the Sainte-Chapelle embodied Gothic perfection.

Like the Sainte-Chapelle on its Île de la Cité in the heart of Paris, the Chapel of Our Lady of Light rests on its island of *ciénega* sand in the heart of Santa Fe. Three sides of its beauty were eclipsed by the sisters' early buildings for almost one hundred years. In 1971 with the demolition of these buildings, an entire generation of tourists and Santa Feans suddenly viewed an heretofore unseen profile of the east end of the chapel. Perhaps the chapel has risen only to be resubmerged, like

Chapel architect Projectus Mouly, ca. 1872. Photo by P. Bagnasco, Santa Fe, N. M. Noël Grenet, Cusset, France.

composer Claude Debussy's *La Cathédrale engloutie* (The Sunken Cathedral), amid the sea of Santa Fe's growth.

It must be declared that the young architect of the chapel, Projectus Mouly, achieved the glorious Gothic by the quintessential expression of chaste design. The proportions and buttresses are heavier than those of Louis IX's private chapel, the Sainte-Chapelle. Nevertheless, quite evident is the "vertical thrust which is carried through by finials and a flèche [the crown-like needle over the apse]" described by one authority of architecture.[18] The heaviness of small windows and the limited light give the chapel a Romanesqueness which leads one to speculate why Gothic was chosen for the sisters' chapel and Romanesque for Lamy's St. Francis Cathedral. Such questions need to be addressed by an in-depth architectural study on the chapel, which has not been done by any of the historic surveys on historical buildings.[19]

The vertical thrust, culminating in peaks and points, gives Gothic its title of "pointed" architecture. The sharp roof slope of the chapel reaches a height of fifty-eight feet to its ridge, covered with a typical turn-of-the-century metal roofing of pressed terneplate (80% lead, 20% tin). Rising another fifteen feet and two inches, the fishscale-shingled *flèche* on the east end is topped with a cross *botonnée* or *trèflee*, whose points terminate in a *trèfoil*. Numerous dormers intercept the roof and are pointed by finials of *fleurs-de-lis*, a three-petaled motif symbolizing the Holy Trinity and the Virgin Mary.[20]

Close examination of the ornate front or west façade of the chapel reveals that it encompasses the dominant characteristic features of Gothic architecture—pointed arches, pinnacles, buttresses, and the rose window. An even closer inspection of the stonework discloses the tight pointing of the stones necessitated by the poor mortar available to stonemasons in the 1870s. Also visible is the etching of the stone done with a brush (a kind of chisel), which was partly decorative and partly to straighten the shape of the stone. The work of the different stonemasons using different chisels is as distinctive as a set of signatures. On the chapel sides, the stone rubble spanning the buttresses, visible in early photographs, was plastered before 1892.

Decorated with the elegant simplicity of a single-pointed leaf motif, the massive nine-and-a-half-foot pine doors of the chapel's entrance rest upon mortared iron pintles supporting strap hinges. Other doors reflect the trèfoil, or trifoliate leaf pattern, found throughout the chapel, symbol in Christian art of the Trinity. A *quatrefoil*, or clover-like motif, occasionally intersperses the trèfoil. Let us open these regal doors and step into the Chapel of Our Lady of Light to gaze the length of the seventy-five-foot nave to receive the first impressions of its interior.

The eye becomes instantly aware of the refined symmetry and scale of the chapel's architectural excellence. Like the Sainte-Chapelle, it is an exquisiteness to be savored, and it commands our total concentration. Viollet-le-Duc tells us, "It is only by lines intelligently combined, forms easily comprehended, and general striking effect, that a deep impression is produced on the mind, and a conception acquires the dignity of a work of art."[21] The heaviness of proportion mentioned earlier is the direct result of the smaller proportion of stained glass in the Chapel of Our Lady of Light than in the Sainte-Chapelle. Missing are the three "walls of glass" separated by thin mullions, or vertical bars, creating the illusion of unlim-

Chapel of Our Lady of Light, ca. 1881. Photo by George C. Bennett, MNM 52452.

ited space and above all, light. The question arises whether the immigrant architect and stonemasons possessed the technical skill to build the fully attenuated Gothic. As we look up, we see a thirty-four-foot-high, four-vault system, ending in the east or altar area in the vaulted apse of three sides. Four arches rest upon five single Corinthian pilasters lining the north and south walls of the nave, crowned with gilded capitals of acanthus leaves, *caulicoli* (*caulis* meaning a stalk) with a honeycomb blossom, four-petaled blossoms with foliage, and guarding the altar, the archangels. The ornately sculptured keystone of the apse with its crockets and archangel, and a small pulley at its base, indicates that a lamp, as mentioned in the early description of the chapel by Lt. John G. Bourke in 1881, indeed could have been suspended here.[22] Two free-standing Corinthian columns with gilded capitals

LORETTO

of acanthus leaves support the choir loft in the rear of the chapel. The choir beam is made of stone.

François-Guillaume Coulloudon, one of the French stonemasons who worked on the chapel, wrote to his wife in Paris in October 1877:

> We are finishing the chapel this winter and it is certain that if I have no work, I shall return to Paris. I want to tell you that I sketched the plans of the chapel by myself. I have found a way to decorate the chapel with pretty niches with the most beautiful molding I was able to imagine. The inside casement windows are formed of beautiful Gothic frames and trim, all made of plaster. I made the designs myself and made my own templates. New Mexico has a very reddish earth but no one realized the worth of it. I found the gypsum myself and had it cured and I assure you that it gave everyone great pleasure when they saw my work on the first moldings. The vicar-in-charge gave me a 20 piastre [$20] bonus for it. The chapel looks like a little jewel. [23]

Guillaume Coulloudon was probably describing the statuary niche in the north wall of the chapel and the elaborate molding of the apsidal area. He also wrote that one of the designs he used resembled a four-leaf clover, the plaster for which he searched all over Santa Fe in order to find the proper kind. The art of running a good mold, without cracks or sags, was passed down from generation to generation, the three sons of Guillaume Coulloudon learning from him as he had learned from his father in France.[24]

Considered an organic part of the Gothic architectural design is the stained glass, an architectural art in itself, existing wholly to fill an aperture and transmit light. If realism was the ultimate pursuit of the Gothic architect, then symbolism was the goal of the stained-glass craftsman. Abbé Suger, father of stained glass, wrote, "The pictures in the windows are there for the purpose of showing simple people, who cannot read the Holy Scriptures, what they must believe."[25] To the early Christian, stained glass represented a visual lesson explaining the Church festivals, the life of Christ, the saints, and other Christian themes. They were to inspire a sense of devotion and faith. Not until the Gothic Revival of the nineteenth century were traditions and techniques of the art of stained glass revived and given new direction.

The windows of the Chapel of Our Lady of Light, while of the finest hand-blown glass (probably of St. Just, France, origin), are treasures but cannot be compared with those of the Sainte-Chapelle, made six centuries earlier.[26] Six *grisaille* (from the French "to paint gray") windows made in 1874 by the Atelier desGrange of Clermont-Ferrand, France, line the chapel nave. Grisaille describes glass that is lightly tinted and painted with foliage pattern or geometrics, and leaded into unique patterns. Surprisingly, the most spectacular grisaille windows are to be found in England not France, often comprising the only kind of window in country churches. Its popularity can be attributed to the fact that it was less expensive than stained glass, allowing windows to be installed while awaiting a generous donor such as Louis IX, known as the patron saint of stained glass. Grisaille originated in the abbeys of the Cistercian Order, which permitted only white glass without figures or crosses.[27]

The two canopied depictions in stained glass to the front of the nave of St. Catherine of Alexandria, patron of girl students and of virgins, holding a palm and a broken spiked wheel at her side, and St. Stanislas, patron of novices, holding a child, were made by desGrange in 1874. In the sanctuary are symbols of the four Evangelists: St. John, the eagle, St. Luke, the winged-ox, St. Matthew, the winged-man, and St. Mark, the winged-lion. These windows of strong sapphire blue hues were made by the duBois Studios of Paris, France, in 1876. Made by the same stained-glass firm were the rear façade window (over-door) and the rose window in the choir loft. In the façade window, the Alpha and Omega, the first and last letters of the Greek alphabet and an ancient symbol of Christ, are in gold on a crimson background. Above this is a quatrefoil of blue and gold. Depicted in the quatrefoil is a true Chi Rho, the Greek letters for "X" and "P," with the Greek

Alter of Chapel of Our Lady of Light, ca. 1890. LMA.

Cross, found in the catacombs of the early Christians. The Chi Rho is the most ancient of sacred monograms for the word *Christ*, and may also be read as the Latin word *pax*, meaning peace.[28] Spanning eight feet, the tracery of the rose window radiates twelve petals, like that of a daisy, symbolic of the Twelve Apostles. Placed in the center is a dazzling gold quatrefoil eye bearing the crowned monogram of the Virgin Mary. Trèfoils intersperse the petal tips.

The fresco in the apse is of gilded red in a design reminiscent of a Byzantine mosaic. Above the altar and on each wall of the three-sided apse are depicted symbolic representatives of the Holy Mass: the Pelican-in-Her-Piety (plucking open her breast, feeding her young with her own blood), symbol of the Redeeming Christ; the Lamb with the Banner of Victory, symbol of the Resurrected Christ; and the Fish and Loaf of Bread, symbol of The Eucharist. Just below the two small sanctuary windows are illuminated monograms, "O S J" and "O S M," representing the Loretto standard of "O Suffering Jesus! O Sorrowful Mary!" The walls of the chapel are done in a gray scored plaster to resemble travertine marble.

Of early twentieth-century design, the ornately carved Gothic altar and communion railing with white marbleized painting were made in Italy. The altar depicts The Last Supper. Fourteen cast marble-dust Stations of the Cross in delicate coloring line the north and south walls of the chapel and are also from Italy.[29]

The Chapel of Our Lady of Light is found to be worthy of Viollet-le-Duc's definition of "a work of art." Its points and arches remain an ever-present symbol to the heroic Sisters of Loretto of their important part in the history of New Mexico. The unmarked grave in Santa Fe's Rosario Cemetery of the young French architect Projectus Mouly deserves a tombstone engraved with the academic title of *doctor lathomorum*—Doctor in Masonry.[30]

CHAPTER 4

THE MYSTERIOUS
SPIRAL STAIRCASE

It grows upward while simultaneously returning again and again to the same point.

Carl Jung, *Man and His Symbols*

VISITORS FROM AROUND THE WORLD come to see the famous spiral staircase of the Chapel of Our Lady of Light in Santa Fe, New Mexico. The widespread fame of the staircase and its legend have surpassed even that of the chapel itself. Notwithstanding the information within these pages regarding the staircase's mysterious carpenter, visitors will continue to come only to find the graceful beauty of the spiral staircase unchanged. Historical truth can neither diminish nor detract from great works of art and devotion.

Legend is often rooted in truth and truth in legend. The parallel of history and legend regarding the spiral staircase emerges as recently discovered facts are examined and we learn of a talented artisan who immigrated to America in search of adventure or a better life. A reclusive French carpenter, who lived and died in anonymity in frontier New Mexico and whose name seldom appears on historical documents, will receive the recognition he never sought during his lifetime.

The Legend

Upon completion of the Chapel of Our Lady of Light in 1878, the Sisters of Loretto found there was no access to their chapel choir loft. They prayed a novena to St. Joseph, the patron saint of carpenters, asking for help. On the final day of the novena a white-bearded man, carrying a tool case and traveling with a donkey, appeared at the convent door seeking work as a carpenter. The sisters employed him immediately. The unknown carpenter began to build a staircase with the skill of a master carpenter. When the carpenter completed the spiral staircase of two 360-degree turns leading to the choir loft, the mysterious man disappeared without being paid for his labor. Thus began the staircase legend which told of an unknown and unpaid carpenter whom the sisters believed to have been St. Joseph.

The History

It is artistically evident that the nineteenth-century workman who built the spiral staircase in the Chapel of Our Lady of Light was a master carpenter. He perceived that no ordinary staircase would suffice for such a fine architectural surrounding. He also recognized that it was a task not simply to build a staircase from point A to point B in a limited space but to do so with accompanying elegance and beauty. The artistic challenge of the staircase in the Chapel of Our Lady of Light demanded the inspiration of the carpenter's art and his faith. In time, he and his spiral accomplishment became cloaked in mystery and legend.

Over the years a list of claimants to the title of "Builder of the Spiral Staircase" included several early Santa Fe carpenters, whose descendants today lay claim to the coveted feat for their ancestry. In 1938 Enrique Sánchez stated that it was his father, Guadalupe, who was one of several workers who worked on the staircase. "Your grandfather was the St. Joseph," Mary Rodriguez was always told by her family. According to the Rodriguez family history, José Antonio Rodriguez made a covenant that if one of his sons reformed, which he did, he would offer his services to the church in return. The name of "A. Rodriguez" appears as a workman for the sisters. "The children were told that José Antonio worked on it very early in the mornings and that he accepted no pay. He did not wish anyone to know about his son and about the promise." Mary Rodriguez believed that Mother Magdalen Hayden was sworn to secrecy, thus making no written record.[1]

Virginia Koplin Stauffer recounted, "My grandfather, Phillip August Hesch, with the help of his son who was my father, John Hesch, built the staircase in Loretto Chapel." Phillip Hesch, born in Bavaria, Germany, learned the carpenter's trade in Ontario, Canada. According to his death notice in the *Santa Fe New Mexican* in 1914:

Hoisting new Hammond Organ to choir loft, 1946. Photo courtesy the author.

It was in 1876 he decided to come to Santa Fe and he at once took an important part in the upbuilding of this city. He was the builder of the Catron Block on the east side of the Plaza, of St. Catherine's Indian School, of three of the buildings of the recent U.S. Indian Industrial School near this city . . . . Mr. Hesch started the first planing mill in Santa Fe. He also put in many of the modern store fronts seen on San Francisco Street.[2]

From the impressive list of accomplishments in Santa Fe, Phillip Hesch possessed the professional ability to have constructed the spiral staircase. However, one death notice failed to mention his work in the Chapel of Our Lady of Light, and the other gives the year 1884 as his arrival in Santa Fe, which the family con-

Phillip August Hesch, ca. 1880s. Builder of the balusters and handrailing of spiral staircase in the Chapel of Our Lady of Light. Courtesy Connie Hesch and John K. Stauffer, Jr.

firms.[3] Nevertheless, the 1946 death notice of John Hesch, Phillip's son, noted that his funeral was held in St. Francis Cathedral "where he carved much of the woodwork," and that he "did some work in Loretto Chapel."[4] A headline gives 1886 as the year of the arrival of John Hesch. By virtue of U.S. Army Lt. John Bourke's account in April 1881 of "a very well built geometrical stairway," Phillip Hesch and his son did not arrive in time to build the stairs.[5] Nevertheless, the Hesches more than likely built the balusters and handrailing of the staircase.

In the July 1887 Day book of the Sisters of Loretto, an entry recorded: "Pd. P. A. Hesch, work, $94.60," and on the following line, "Rec'd of do [ditto] in labor, $94.60, he still owes us $17.70."[6] Phillip Hesch apparently traded his labor for the 1886 or 1887 tuition of his five daughters, Carrie, Laura, Minnie, Hattie, and Helena, in the Academy of Our Lady of Light by building the balusters and handrailing for the sisters. Thus the sisters climbed the staircase, some on their hands and knees without a handrailing, for approximately five or six years. John Hesch and Sons established a blind (shutter) and sash mill in 1887 near the Santuario de Guadalupe "for turning out all sorts of mouldings, fancy castings, stair railing, etc."[7]

The family history of Frederic Grace, age fifty years in 1880, tells of his work on the chapel. Grace, whose descendants live in Santa Fe today, was a carpenter from Pennsylvania and had two sons, Hipolito and Julian, who were also carpenters.[8]

(preceding page) Front view of the Chapel of
Our Lady of Light, 1993. Photo by Mary Peck.
(above) Capitals of pilasters of the chapel.
Photo by Len Bouché.
(right) IV Station of the Cross.
Photo by Len Bouché.
(below) View from choir loft looking down
spiral staircase. Photo by Len Bouché.

(above left) Saint Catherine of Alexandria, stained glass window by Atelier desGrange, Clermont-Ferrand. Photo by Mary Peck.
(above center) Stained glass over-door window by du Bois Studios, Paris. Photo by Len Bouché.
(above right) Saint Stanislas, stained glass window by Atelier desGrange, Clermont-Ferrand, France. Photo by Mary Peck.
(below left) Stained glass rose window by du Bois Studios, Paris. Photo by Len Bouché.
(below right) Grisaille window of north wall of the chapel. Photo by Mary Peck.
(following page) The Loretto Chapel Spiral Staircase. Photo by Len Bouché.

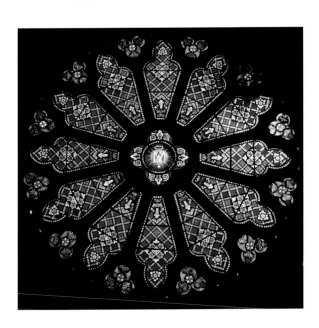

There are countless other staircase carpenter stories. A carpenter and gambler named "Sawdust Charlie" also worked on the staircase, according to the descendants of his family. His real name was Charles Frederick Yardman; he had come to Santa Fe from Germany. The Sisters of Loretto took him under their care despite his reputation as a "bunko steerer." A notice posted in Las Vegas, New Mexico, listing the name of Sawdust Charlie along with that of the famed Billy the Kid warned certain roving gamblers that they would be invited to a "Grand Necktie Party, the expense of which will be borne by 100 substantial citizens."[9]

The most publicized claimant, however, captured front-page headlines of the *New Mexican* of February 26, 1970, in a story by reporter Ron Longto. The headlines read, "Miracle Staircase' [*sic*] carpenter identity revealed." The article began:

The ancient and beautiful legend of the Famous Staircase in the Chapel of Our Lady of Light in Santa Fe remains intact today although the identity of the mysterious builder has been unveiled. . . . It was never openly said, but there were whispers and strong beliefs that the gray-haired old man who offered his services to the sisters in building the staircase was really St. Joseph.

The newspaper article quoted the story of Oscar Hadwiger from Pueblo, Colorado, which told that the master carpenter who built the staircase was Yohon (Johann) L. Hadwiger, Oscar's grandfather from Vienna, Austria.[10] According to Oscar, his father, John Hadwiger, ran away from home and came to America as a boy of twelve years in 1872. Like many other immigrants of the time, John traveled west to prospering Pueblo. When his parents in Austria learned of his whereabouts, the father, Yohon, came to the United States in late 1877 or early 1878 to bring the son home to Austria. Upon finding that his son wished to remain in this country, Yohon Hadwiger decided to tour the area; he discovered the gold and silver rush, which was going full tilt in Colorado. "When my grandfather returned to Pueblo from Ouray and Silverton, he told my father he had built some stairs in a church at Santa Fe, but did not finish them," related Oscar Hadwiger. Yohon returned to Austria, never again to travel to the United States. Oscar also told that his grandfather never returned to Santa Fe for his pay.

To document his case, Oscar Hadwiger produced a rough sketch of a spiral staircase showing thirty-two steps of a double helix. The sketch purportedly was made by Yohon Hadwiger in 1878. Over the years and as therapy against arthritis, Oscar himself built several models of the spiral staircase, proving that he was a master carpenter like his grandfather. Albeit, Oscar Hadwiger established an outstanding reputation of his own in Colorado with his wood artistry. Hadwiger carved and inlaid well over eight hundred pieces, from spiral staircases to musical instruments.[11]

Oscar's friendship with the Sisters of Loretto in Santa Fe began five years before the article appeared in the *New Mexican*. He wrote to the sisters as well as gave many interviews for various publications throughout the United States. In the fall of 1965, Oscar Hadwiger first visited the sisters and their Chapel of Our Lady of Light. The question arose concerning the identity of the staircase builder; one of the sisters asked him if he had built it. This sent Oscar home to Pueblo with fleeting thoughts from his childhood when he seemed to recall his father telling him a story about his grandfather. He sent a letter to the sisters telling them that he believed the itinerant carpenter with the burro who built the staircase had been his grandfather, Yohon, from Austria.

Predictably, the letter hit the sisters like a bolt out of the blue, and the mother superior shot back a tersely worded reply:

> We enjoyed reading your reminiscences of the pioneering days of this frontier, and the idea you developed with regard to the man who built the Stairs as being your Grandfather.
>
> After all, it is just an imaginary statement on your part that the man who built the Stairs was your Grandfather—a fine builder of Stairs—but to make a definite statement without proof that it was your Grandfather would be an evasion of the truth since Mother Magdalen herself wrote

Loretto Academy choir on spiral staircase, ca. 1960. Lord Studio, MNM 14722.

to the Mother Superior making the statement that she did not know the man just a short time after he disappeared. Even if you had proof we could not accept it since there is not a Sister living today who could identify him or give a description of him.

I am sure we would run into difficulties if we allowed such a report to be published in the newspaper. For instance, there is a family living here who are descendants of a man who claims he worked on the Chapel at the time the stairs were built.

We therefore ask that you do not proceed with the publication of any such idea as we could not verify it and you would be accused of fraud.[12]

Obviously shaken by the sisters' stern reprimand of his claim, Oscar Hadwiger apologized in his unassuming manner. He simply had not realized how his sudden announcement might upset the sisters, agreeing with them that he could not prove anything. After Oscar's first visit to Santa Fe and in an attempt to validate his claim, he requested the sisters to delegate an impossible job for him to complete, signing his letters "Old Oscar." Old Oscar wooed and won the hearts of the Sisters of Loretto, and they apologetically responded:

We are mailing to you today a copy of the Loretto Magazine which has just been received. It is a co-incident that it should have come just at this time to persuade you there are no ill feelings between us. Our letter may have been a little harsh and we are sorry. Our intention was to prevent you from having any difficulty about making a statement that might not be wholly convincing. . . .

It surely would be interesting to see the plans for the circular stairs made by your Grandfather in those far-off days.

Many people have seen the Miniature Stair-replicas of the Famous Stairs, and have greatly admired your skill and ingenuity. We haven't come across any other "impossible jobs." Perhaps we haven't had time to think about them. We will get in touch with you should anything of this nature come to our attention.

Please accept our apology for being so abrupt, and thank you for your patience and kind consideration.[13]

Oscar continued to write to the Sisters of Loretto in Santa Fe and to give numerous interviews with various magazines. Unquestionably, the Hadwigers of Pueblo, Colorado, knew how to build staircases. Talented Oscar expressed the fear that the spiral stairs in the chapel might collapse in time because of the dead grain of the wood, which could be compared to the folding and unfolding of a pulp newspaper's fibers. He offered a solution for leveling the spiral staircase, which had settled seven inches or more through the years. His suggestion was carried out by the construction crew of the Inn at Loretto ten years later during the chapel restoration, although the Inn at Loretto people never knew of Oscar's suggestion. The staircase was gently raised by an hydraulic jack and a cement footing poured under it. Until that time, the staircase rested precariously on a single floor joist.

The Sisters of Loretto once wrote to Oscar, "Your 75-year old secret has become the source of much attention or bewilderment through the years." Old Oscar Hadwiger and the good sisters ended their correspondence on that prophetic statement. After years of research, the author could neither prove nor disprove the Hadwiger claim. From time to time, other families suggest a new name to be added to the list of carpenters.

Over time the public became more and more aware of the spiral staircase, particularly after Robert Ripley drew it. The drawing appeared in 1939 newspapers across the country in his "Believe It or Not!" Ripley illustrated the staircase a second time in 1956.[14] With this added publicity, the staircase became famous as more and more tourists began to include the Chapel of Our Lady of Light as a part of their historic Santa Fe tour. The chapel history remains linked with the history of nineteenth-century Santa Fe and the arrival of the French priests and European workmen brought by Archbishop Jean-Baptiste Lamy. The spiraling staircase and its legend are a favorite tourist attraction today in Santa Fe.

François-Jean Rochas, Carpenter and Rancher
(1843–1894)

After many years of mystery, an elusive Frenchman named François-Jean Rochas has been documented as the carpenter of the legendary spiral staircase in the Chapel of Our Lady of Light. While other carpenters may have assisted him during the construction, Rochas was called its builder by his friend Quintus Monier, contractor of St. Francis Cathedral in Santa Fe, who also worked on the chapel.[15] On January 5, 1895, the following brief paragraph appeared in the *Santa Fe New Mexican:*

> A letter from Las Cruces to Mr. Quintus Monier, of date yesterday, states that Frank Rochas was found dead at his ranch house near La Luz, a few days ago. His friends believe that he was assassinated as previous attempts have been made. He was a Frenchman, and was favorably known in Santa Fe as an expert worker in wood. He build [*sic*] the handsome staircase in the Loretto chapel and at St. Vincent sanitarium.[16]

The statement by Monier was a sad reminder to the Catholic community of Santa Fe that François-Jean Rochas and Mother Magdalen Hayden had died a brief two months apart, she in October and he in December 1894. Mother Magdalen, superior during the building of the chapel, may have been the Sister of Loretto who communicated with the talented Rochas on a day-to-day basis during the staircase construction, first-hand knowledge about the master carpenter dying with her.

Some Loretto Sisters today tend to believe that French-speaking Francesca Lamy, the archbishop's niece and the second mother superior, was an intermediary (Rochas spoke little or no English). What is now known about the carpenter and his solitary personality, the result of early habits and possible training as a *compagnon* (a French artisan brotherhood who are celibate), would probably rule out a woman as a liaison.[17] The person giving instructions to Rochas, if indeed any were necessary, needed specific knowledge. In the author's opinion, it was Quintus Monier or a French priest. As we learned earlier, artisan Guillaume Coulloudon wrote to his wife that he had received a bonus for his work from the "vicar-in-charge."

Other French artisans living in Santa Fe at the time also knew and dined with Rochas at the bishop's table during the construction of the several major Catholic buildings in the nineteenth century. These major buildings were: Chapel of Our Lady of Light (1873–78); Loretto Academy (1881); St. Francis Cathedral (1869–87); and the Sisters of Charity Sanitarium (1878–81). There were also large private residences being built.[18] Rochas's countryman and fellow artisan Quintus Monier considered the death of Rochas to be of particular interest to Santa Feans despite the stair builder's ten-year or more absence from northern New Mexico. Monier probably held the work of the master carpenter in high esteem.[19]

Why had historians failed to uncover the name of the carpenter François-Jean Rochas during the century and more the legend endured? One elderly New Mexican told the author that there were indeed those who knew the carpenter's name but who did not wish to betray the legend. The staircase builder's identity was of little interest to the public until his accomplishment reached legendary proportions, sometime during the early decades of the twentieth century. By then, those who had known or worked with Rochas were dead. A chapter of history inevitably dies with each passing generation, and oral history often becomes a variation of historical fact. We must surmise that this was the case regarding the spiral staircase in Loretto Chapel.[20]

To trace the year-to-year whereabouts of such a man as Rochas challenges the researcher's acumen. It can be documented, nevertheless, that in 1881 Rochas worked for the sisters in Santa Fe. An entry in the Loretto sisters' Day book reads:

Marzo de 1881

> 12   Paid for wood   1.60
>
> —Mr. Rochas for N. [New] School   150.00[21]

The above bookkeeping entry records Rochas as working for the Sisters of Loretto in March of 1881, three years following the chapel completion in 1878. The entry gives us other clues as well, such as the information that between 1878 and 1881 the sisters reached the choir loft by ladder only—wearing long habits. Early New Mexico church-building tradition accommodated men rather than women; the Sisters of Loretto were the first religious women in New Mexico. The floor-length habits worn by them made ladder-climbing dangerous, if not impossible.

The $150 payment to Rochas indicated work in the new Loretto Academy building, completed in 1881, immediately north of the chapel. In addition, the March 1881 entry possibly indicates that construction on the chapel spiral staircase was completed by that date and that Rochas was at work on another project for the sisters in the adjacent building. Documentation of any earlier payment to carpenter Rochas for construction of the spiral staircase could not be found in the sisters' books. It may have been part of a lump sum paid to Archbishop Lamy, as mentioned earlier, or that payment to the carpenter was made in France prior to the staircase arrival.[22]

For over a century, Rochas's name remained a mystery to researchers. No historical link between an eccentric French hermit ranching in a remote area of southern New Mexico to the unknown master carpenter of the spiral staircase in northern New Mexico was ever established. At Dog Canyon, near Alamogordo, New Mexico, the man named François-Jean Rochas (called Frank or Frenchy) achieved his place in nineteenth-century New Mexico history as the irascible neighbor of a well-known rancher named Oliver Lee. In the late 1900s Oliver Lee played a prominent role in a turbulent era of cattle rustlers and unsolved murders following on the heels of the Lincoln County War era of Billy the Kid.[23] So, as a result of time and circumstance, the name of François-Jean Rochas as the spiral staircase carpenter of Loretto Chapel remained undocumented between 1895 and 1995.[24] Once the Santa Fe-Dog Canyon connection was established, other corroborating clues added credence to the Rochas identity as that of the staircase builder.

The important historical link in solving the staircase mystery was the names of the French workmen which Rochas mentions shortly before his death. Upon the discovery of Rochas's body in late December 1894, three unmailed letters dated December 23, 1894, were found on a table in his crude rock cabin at Dog Canyon. Two letters were written to his brother and sister in France, but most importantly, a third was addressed to Q. Monier in Santa Fe. All three letters were written in French. The following is a translation of the Rochas letter to Monier:

La Luz le 23 December 1894

Mr. Q. Monier   Santa Fé

Dear Friend

You will certainly be surprised when you receive this letter to see that I am thinking of you. However I assure you that I think of you sometimes. I have had news of you and of Mr. Baptiste Lamy through Mr. [Numa] Reymond. I have had none from [Etienne] Lacassagne and I should like to have some. I am writing you also because I have a little need of you. I do not write English and my handwriting is bad. I should like to correspond with the Surveyor General, whose station is at Santa Fe. The land on which I live is not surveyed and I should like to know how to act to get it surveyed and I have been thinking that you would be able to get me the necessary information. I think he will need to know in what township and section I am situated. Surveyors have passed by here several times. The last one left me a plat of my place with the number of the township and the number of the quarter-section. But I cannot find it and I must certainly have lost it. The name of the surveyor I cannot give you but it will be easy for you to find it. He lives in Santa Fe as does his father, who is also a surveyor. The young man stammers a good deal. He must have it

Etienne Lacassagne, ca. 1880s. One of the French artisans who built the Chapel of Our Lady of Light. Courtesy Lacassagne family.

on his books, I am certain. The name of the place is Dog Canyon. I hope that this will not give you too much trouble. I think you will not be too busy at this time. Here it is still warm. It has frozen a little but hardly enough for one to see. Almost all the trees still have their leaves. I hope you have continued in good health and that you have had plenty of work; the same for Lacassagne, of whom I hope you can give me news. As for me, it is always the same thing. I am just the same, except for a few gray hairs. I feel well except for this miserable catarrh in the head and also in the stomach. Well, some day one will die, and that will relieve us of all these maladies. Send me news also of Mr. Baptiste Lamy. I think perhaps you may know these people—I mean the surveyors. That will make the business easier. Since we are at the end of the year, I conclude by wishing you a happy New Year and remain always your friend

Frank Rochas [25]

"Q. Monier, Baptiste Lamy [Archbishop Jean-Baptiste Lamy], and Lacassagne" were prominent French people in the history of the Catholic building projects in Santa Fe during the 1870s and 1880s. Interestingly, Archbishop Lamy had been dead six years at the time Rochas wrote his 1894 letter to Monier inquiring about the prelate. It is curious that Frank Rochas had not learned of Lamy's death from one of his French friends in Las Cruces. Intermittently, Rochas traveled westward by cart across the sandy Tularosa Basin to buy supplies and to enjoy camaraderie with his French-speaking friends. The 1894 letter illustrates the isolated life led by Rochas at Dog Canyon.

Known historical facts about Rochas's earlier life before his arrival in the United States are limited to his genealogy and family oral history; no member of his immediate family survives today. François-Jean Rochas was born September 22, 1843, in Vif, Department of Isère, France, where the Rochas name appears in the early seventeenth-century Hautes-Alpes. The son of François-Charles Rochas and Anne-Victoire Chaulon, François-Jean was the eldest of four children. His brother and sisters were: Victoire-Josephine (1846–?); Joseph-Charles (1849–?); and Marie-Pauline (1859–?).

Vif is a small town approximately six kilometers south of Grenoble in southeastern France.[26] Frank, as he was later called, immigrated to the United States from the alpine village of Uriol which overlooked nearby Vif. A vine pest had spread to Vercors vineyards, the apparent reason for Uriol's eventual abandonment. Similar to his life in New Mexico, Rochas lived in France in relative isolation in Uriol.

United States immigration records show that on September 14, 1880, a Rochas (no given name) is listed as an "Agent" on the manifest of the S. S. *St. Laurent*, a commercial cargo vessel from (Le) Harve, France. Nineteen-year-old Levis (Lewis?) Reymond, a clerk and perhaps a relative of Numa Reymond, New Mexico-Swiss entrepreneur and French-speaking friend of Rochas in Las Cruces, is also aboard the *St. Laurent*. A conjecture has been made by a French compagnon suggesting that the spiral staircase was cut in France, Rochas accompanying it to New York on the *St. Laurent*. It would have been shipped from New York to Lamy, New Mexico, fourteen miles south of Santa Fe and the point of arrival of the railroad tracks, under the supervision of carpenter François-Jean Rochas. Whereupon, Rochas proceeded to assemble it, perhaps in the workshop across the street from the chapel.

The arrival of the Atcheson, Topeka & Santa Fe Railroad in Lamy in January of 1880 dramatically hastened the long journey from New York to Santa Fe.[27] With the arrival of Rochas during late September 1880, we may now surmise that construction of the spiral staircase in Loretto Chapel commenced in early October 1880 and was completed by April 1881, the earliest known staircase description. A point of disagreement among carpenters and staircase aficionados today, however, has been the construction time factor—that a carpenter could not have built a staircase of such complex design in so short a time as October 1880 to April 1881. So the theory that the staircase was cut in France appears logical.[28]

Other Frenchmen already in New Mexico by the year 1880 surely played a key role in the life of the new émigré Rochas. Their established contacts with influential Santa Fe citizens, plus their acquired knowledge of English, would have been indispensable to him. Rochas might even have traveled with them during the course of other construction projects in other places.

During his move southward, Rochas possibly accompanied Quintus Monier to Socorro, where the contractor was granted a license in November 1883 to build a restaurant.[29] The arrival of the railroad had brought considerable construction throughout the state—excellent wages awaited a master carpenter. Coincidentally, in 1883 the Sisters of Loretto were also established in the southern New Mexico towns of Socorro and Las Cruces.[30]

The question arises why Rochas chose to leave his friends and live alone at Dog Canyon, but it must be remembered this had been his lifestyle in France. The narrow canyon crevice, and its precious water, had been used since the time of the sixteenth-century Spaniards as an escape route for Apache raiding parties returning to the safety of the cool Sacramento Mountains. Early Spaniards had called it *Cañon del Perro* after finding a stray dog wandering in the steep gorge. Rochas no doubt heard of land available for homesteading via the grapevine of the French clergy of Las Cruces, Fathers Andres Eschallier and Pierre Lassaigne; they traveled between Las Cruces and Santa Fe. Rochas may have traveled to the Dog Canyon area with his Swiss friend Numa Reymond, who with another partner in 1884, held a supply and freighting contract between Las Cruces and the Mescalero Apache Reservation.[31]

Rochas knew another Frenchman in southern New Mexico—Theodore Rouault, a former French-priest-turned-merchant, who married a Loretto novice. Rouault was administrator of Rochas's estate in 1895. Father Pierre Lassaigne of St. Genevieve's in Las Cruces was the priest for a time in Tularosa, New Mexico, a few miles north of La Luz, the nearest village to Dog Canyon. As an itinerant priest serving several churches, Lassaigne occasionally traveled the sandy plains to La Luz to conduct mass. No matter how Rochas learned of Dog Canyon, he had to be extraordinarily brave or foolhardy to live so very isolated, directly in the path of marauding Apache Indians. Furthermore, the Frenchman would have had to learn to coexist with the Mescalero Apaches or lose his self-described, graying scalp.

The name of Frank Rochas appears in La Luz, Doña Ana County, in June 1886, when he lists himself as owning property valued at a substantial $2,680. How and when he accumulated this sizable sum of money is unknown, possibly from lucrative carpentry work in Santa Fe. A fellow French workman named François-Guillaume Coulloudon wrote to his wife in Paris that his construction pay in Santa Fe was $50 a month. The Moulys, father and son architects of St. Francis Cathedral and Loretto Chapel, accumulated $5,200 in four years from Santa Fe building projects.[32]

Lacking information of how and when he arrived, we know that Rochas had established his claim by 1886 at Dog Canyon, eight miles south of Alamogordo and east of White Sands in the Tularosa Basin. Here, he spent the remaining years of his life. The only woodworking in Dog Canyon, attributed possibly to Rochas, in southern New Mexico, still remains—that of the window frames of the ranch house of Oliver Lee, his closest neighbor. Rochas also built with rock.

From 1886 until December 1894, when Frank Rochas was found dead (called a suicide by the La Luz coroner), what little is known about New Mexico's evasive Frenchman can be documented in public tax records, the census, and probate court records. Rather convincing evidence can be found that the Frenchy of Dog Canyon

Altar and nave with electric lights, ca. 1965. LMA.

was indeed capable of building the spiral staircase in Loretto Chapel. Among his possessions are listed a number of sophisticated woodworking tools which might have been employed by a master carpenter constructing a spiral staircase.[33]

At Dog Canyon, Rochas built a one-room rock cabin for himself with a spectacular westward view toward Las Cruces, across the White Sands Monument, today the site of missile launches and shuttle landings. Rocks used to build the eight-by-eight-foot cabin exhibit unusual geological character and size, the northwest cornerstone weighing several hundred pounds. In this rustic abode Frenchy had prepared well, or so he thought, for the contingencies of living alone with violence and thievery lurking nearby. He incorporated an interior, ground-level escape route out the back of the small cabin. Also in the cabin wall was a secret cache for money or gold. The self-reliant Frank Rochas had conveniently cached a gun elsewhere for any unexpected, life-threatening encounters when he was away from his stone abode.

Besides his rock cabin, Frank Rochas constructed several extraordinary rock walls during his years of residency at Dog Canyon. With Herculean strength, Rochas built stone walls at steep thirty-degree angles on the canyon face, still visible today, to prevent his cattle from straying. He also built aqueducts to deliver Dog Canyon spring water to the basin floor. Unquestionably, the shrewdest accomplishment of the Frenchman was the acquisition of the most valuable of southwestern assets—water—for his cattle and fruit trees.

The reclusive Rochas met the test of his preparedness in 1886. He discovered that a cowhand in his employ had stolen from him; he then swore out a warrant in La Luz for the culprit's arrest. A would-be Billy the Kid named John Morris (Morrison), filled with revenge, shot Frenchy, who managed to struggle back to his rock room to lie in wait for Morris's return.[34] When Morris opened the front door to the cabin, Frenchy shot him in the arm. The wounded ranch hand hightailed it up the steep Dog Canyon to the sanctity of the Sacramento Mountains, where he was trapped by some ranchers and brought back to justice.

Young John Morris was sent to the New Mexico State Penitentiary in Santa Fe with a sentence of three years for assault with intent to murder. He soon escaped and was recaptured. That was not the last of his escapades. In 1912 Morris occupied the penitentiary a second time for larceny of cattle but was ultimately released.[35]

The life of Frank Rochas, the rancher, proved to be in constant danger as he labored in the out-of-doors improving his ranch and herding his cattle. Apparently, ten years passed without another incident until December 1894, when Rochas was found dead in his cabin by Dan Fitchett, a cowhand of rancher Oliver Lee. As mentioned earlier, the coroner ruled the Rochas death a suicide, and his body was buried in the Nuestra Señora de La Luz Cemetery in La Luz, New Mexico.[36] His seemingly unquestioned death resembled others of the turbulent era in southern New Mexico during the last decades of the 1800s.

Restoration of rock cabin of François-Jean Rochas at mouth of Dog Canyon. Photo by author.

For almost a century, a crude wooden board marked the remote grave of the man whom many in northern New Mexico believed to have been St. Joseph. Today, a gray granite stone is chiseled with the following inscription: "Gunned Down at His Rock Cabin in Dog Canyon." The mystery surrounding the life and death of François-Jean Rochas, the carpenter, also known as Frank Rochas, the rancher, continues. It is but another nineteenth-century New Mexico mystery yet to be totally solved.

Recent tombstone of François-Jean Rochas in Nuestra Señora de la Luz Cemetary. Photo by author.

CHAPTER 5

THE HARMONIUM

By Appointment to the Emperor.

Alexandre-François Debain

THE NAME "HARMONIUM" was first patented August 9, 1840, by Alexandre-François Debain (1802–1877) of Paris, France, builder of the 1867 instrument in the Chapel of Our Lady of Light.[1] Debain, whose patent read, "By Appointment to the Emperor," sued and won his legal claim to the title "Inventeur de l' harmonium."[2] Later this name generically denoted all kinds of keyboard instruments whose sound is produced by free-vibrating metal reeds or tongues set in motion by wind forced from two pedal-operated bellows. Another name used by other French builders of similar instruments is *"orgue expressif."*[3] Thus the names harmonium and organ remain inextricably confused in the musical instrument nomenclature.

As a musical instrument the harmonium possesses a greater capacity for expressiveness than its better-known rival, the American reed organ. Peculiar to the harmonium alone is the stop called "Expression."[4] Another characteristic is a divided register between e' to f' in the center of the keyboard (just above middle c) that enables the treble half to gain dynamic independence from the bass half. It allows a melody, whether in bass or soprano, to soar over its accompaniment.

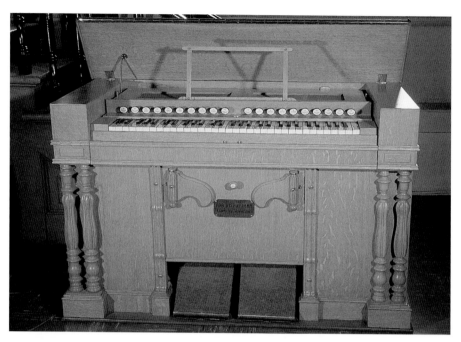

Alexandre-François Debain harmonium (after restoration), ca.1867. Photo by Len Bouché.

Alexandre-François Debain, an inventive genius, also built mechanical pianos and harmoniums, some with transposing keyboards, that could be played either from a keyboard or by pinned cylinders, perforated cardboard strips or metal discs.[5] Some of his instruments survive today in major museum collections of Europe and the United States.[6] Of added musical significance here, however, is that the Debain harmonium of the Chapel of Our Lady of Light may be heard in its original 1878 acoustical environment. What a rare privilege.

An extremely popular instrument for home and church music-making, the harmonium and its timbre attracted many musicians, important nineteenth- and twentieth-century composers such as Richard Strauss, Antonin Dvoràk, Arnold Schoenberg, and Sigfrid Karg-Elert. Its musical repertoire ranks as substantial and unique.[7]

Two years after her arrival in Santa Fe, Mother Superior Magdalen Hayden wrote to a friend in 1854:

LORETTO

Debain medallion and stops of harmonium.
Photo by Mary Peck.

Plaque of Debain harmonium. Photo
by Mary Peck.

We now have a seraphine or small organ for our chapel. The price is $150, but our boarders gave $91 toward the purchase. It has a sweet tone and I am very much pleased with it. . . . Now I hope that we shall have music in our chapel at least each Sunday.[8]

The year in which Mother Magdalen wrote this preceded the arrival of the Debain harmonium and the building of the new chapel by over twenty-five years. Organ music was important to the sisters. Both Bishop Lamy and the sisters came to Santa Fe from traditions steeped in organ literature, and any other sound in the church evoked secular associations to nineteenth-century Catholics and Protestants alike, as we shall soon see.[9] Religious services today resound with guitars and violins to a rhythmical beat once thought inappropriate.

On August 16, 1866, Mother Magdalen penned the first major expenditure for the new chapel, *"Por el Señor Obispo, dad a él para traemos 1 organito se de Francia, $400."* [10] Another Day book entry that same year records, "Bp. left Aug. 27 for Europe. M. M. gave him $400 to buy an organ, crucifix, 1 painting, and materials for artificial flowers."[11]

Bishop Lamy often shopped in Paris for the sisters on his trips to Europe.[12] To order their organ he would have called at the imposing five-story atelier on the Rue de Lafayette of the distinguished musical instrument builder Alexandre-François Debain, where he would have described the strenuous demands to be met.[13] It must be an instrument of quality workmanship, the case of oak to withstand the dryness of New Mexico's air and strong enough to survive a lengthy journey from Paris to Santa Fe via boat, train, and wagon; its volume and intonation must suit projected dimensions of the new chapel for accompaniment of the Mass; it must be compact to fit a small choir loft, and it must also fit the sisters' budget.[14]

Several years earlier Bishop Lamy shopped for an organ, but not in Paris. In a letter written in 1851, seven months after his arrival in Santa Fe, Lamy indicated his preference for the more familiar resonant organ tones to accompany the Mass rather than traditional New Mexico violins and guitars. He purchased a small organ from a friendly Protestant minister.[15] This change of instrumentation for the Mass also prompted a change of musicians and new repertoire, prophetic of other Lamy reforms that would forever permeate the Catholic annals of nineteenth-century New Mexico history.

According to more than one account, local musicians often followed native dancers from the *fandango* the night before to early Mass the next morning, carrying with them their instruments and tunes whose tempi varied little for the living or dead.[16] *Fandango* dancers, though winded and fatigued from the previous evening's entertainment, more than likely composed the church choir.[17] While in Santa Fe, a Lt. J. W. Abert wrote in his 1846 journal:

> I was much surprised with the manners of the Mexicans at a funeral. They marched with great rapidity through the streets near the church, with a band of music. The instruments were principally violins, and these were played furiously, sending forth wild raging music . . . and the mourners talked and laughed gaily, which seemed to me most strange. I was told, too, that the tunes played were the same as those which sounded at the fandango.[18]

Susan Magoffin, an American woman who crossed the Santa Fe Trail in 1846, confirms Lt. Abert's observation as she describes her "first lesson in Catholicism" after attending Mass in a Santa Fe church. Magoffin's puritan background became apparent as she wrote:

> Their music consisted of a violin, which all the time they continued to tune, and a thumming gingling guitar; the same tunes they had the other night at the fandango, were played. It is a strange mode of worship to a protestant who has been raised to regard the Sabbath with strictest piety, not even to think of a dancing tune on a violin, let the hearing of it alone.[19]

The journey Lamy embarked upon in 1866 ultimately took him to Rome as courier for the Second Plenary Council at Baltimore, which he stopped to attend before leaving the American continent. Not only did he carry with him the Sisters of Loretto's $400 but minutes of the Council's meetings discussing proposals for the creation of apostolic vicariates for Colorado and Arizona.[20] Delivering the minutes to Rome, Bishop Lamy returned to Paris for three months, but any pursuit of an organ or harmonium or its eventual arrival in Santa Fe escaped documentation.[21] An 1877 *Revista Católica* of Las Vegas, New Mexico, notes a ceremony of great beauty held in the new Chapel of Our Lady of Light, remarking that the melodious voices of the sisters were accompanied by the organ. Or did the writer mean a harmonium?[22]

One sister recalled that it was not all that easy to sound melodious. In her memoirs Mother Bernard Doyle, who made her novitiate in Santa Fe in 1880, told of her musical struggles on the harmonium. Her teacher was Mother Francesca Lamy, the musical niece of Archbishop J. B. Lamy, who became the second mother superior of the Convent of Our Lady of Light.

> Will I ever forget several organ lessons Mother Francesca gave me— Never! The organ at Santa Fe is of French make, hence rather hard to manipulate and bring out the music, then too, I was supposed to cling to

the keys and not use the piano touch. But my touch down on the pedals and another on the keys seemed rather difficult for me—the feet would go down and the hands jump the keys—then Mother's hand would come down on mine for a touch down. After a hard struggle, hands and feet learned to make a correct touch down. The first time I played a hymn during Mass was when [I] was still a novice—naturally timid before the Sisters. I made a very poor presentation. Mother pumped with one foot and with her hand tried to keep my hands on the keyboard. Finally the goal was made and I really learned to play the organ very well.[23]

A practiced Sister Bernard, her confidence bolstered after several years of playing, told Sister Orline Tefler, a 1918 arrival to Santa Fe, "You sounded like you were ploughing a field," as she played the harmonium.[24] When the expression stop is engaged, one does have the feeling of ploughing a field when playing, and the need of a bench screwed to the floor because the pedal resistance is so great.

Just when the sisters first began to learn to play the harmonium and master its technique, we cannot be sure. A chronology of names penciled inside the Debain harmonium gives inconclusive evidence of the exact year of its arrival in Santa Fe. The change from French to English by the repairmen indicates between 1883 and 1886.

Paris 1867 Edouard Ege
Reparé par Edouard Ege - Juillet 1883
Repaired August Wehrle 1886 [25]
Repaired J. H. Thomas - March 25, 1907, Denver, Colo.

The name "Lemire" is stamped into the wood of the reed pan with a penciled line through it and "*Preparé De*" written just below. Carved into the case top are the serial numbers 18358 from around 1882–83 (restruck over the original number of

17372, the 2 somewhat obscured, 1867) on the left side and 9853 on the right. Below the keyboard an engraved brass plaque declares "For Bishop Lamy, Santa-Fé, New-Mexico."

Another sixty years passed as the French harmonium remained in the choir loft of the Chapel of Our Lady of Light. Unplayable from decrepitude and in need of extensive repairs, it fell from musical grace, and a Hammond organ replaced it in 1946; an electric organ needs no foot pumping.[26] Debain's patented invention disappeared into historic limbo during the next twenty-two years.

In finale to a 166-year saga, Loretto Academy closed its massive Victorian doors in 1968, and the sisters' historic property beside the old Santa Fe Trail was sold in 1971.[27] Stored furnishings and paintings were disposed of and the archbishop given the harmonium. Lowered from the choir loft, the Debain instrument was retired to a basement in the Palace of the Governors, joining other forgotten memorabilia as a part of the Santa Fe Archdiocesan Collection. No date records its arrival in the Museum of New Mexico.

By 1975 Paul Horgan's Pulitzer Prize-winning biography of the life of Archbishop Jean-Baptiste Lamy, entitled *Lamy of Santa Fe*, reached publication. Horgan's vivid description of the Debain instrument aroused this writer's interest, and a search ensued. Once found, the harmonium and its restoration brought about an unprecedented loan agreement between the Historic Santa Fe Foundation, by then administrator of the chapel as well as financier of the Debain project, and the archbishop, owner of the harmonium. Negotiations consumed years, and in the early summer of 1980 the author drove the harmonium from Santa Fe to Ft. Worth, Texas, to be conserved by the organ firm of Roy Redman. Again in limbo, the instrument remained there another year before actual work began—the result of yet one more unforeseen technicality unresolved.

On a cold January day in 1982, Alexandre-François Debain's harmonium made its second trip down the old Santa Fe Trail and was precariously hoisted to its historical place atop the spiral staircase in the Chapel of Our Lady of Light. Posterity noted its arrival this time. Rededication ceremonies conducted by the Historic Santa Fe Foundation, in collaboration with the Archdiocese of Santa Fe, marked Sunday, July 4, 1982, as a harmonious occasion. Rich tones of Antonín Dvořák's *Bagatelles* for harmonium and string trio composed in 1878, the year of the chapel's dedication, awakened all who heard to an extraordinary sound worthy of a French emperor.[28]

APPENDIX A
CHAPEL DRAWINGS

THE AUTHOR WISHES TO THANK Ted Davalos, Dane Andes, and Tom McCollum for their permission to use the drawings rendered by them in the 1960s while students of Bainbridge Bunting at the University of New Mexico.

While it was not feasible to do a complete remeasuring of the chapel before publication, the drawings were checked for rough accuracy. To date, no measured drawings have been made of the chapel by any survey of historical buildings. The illustrations in the appendix are for general reference only and not intended to be definitive measured drawings.

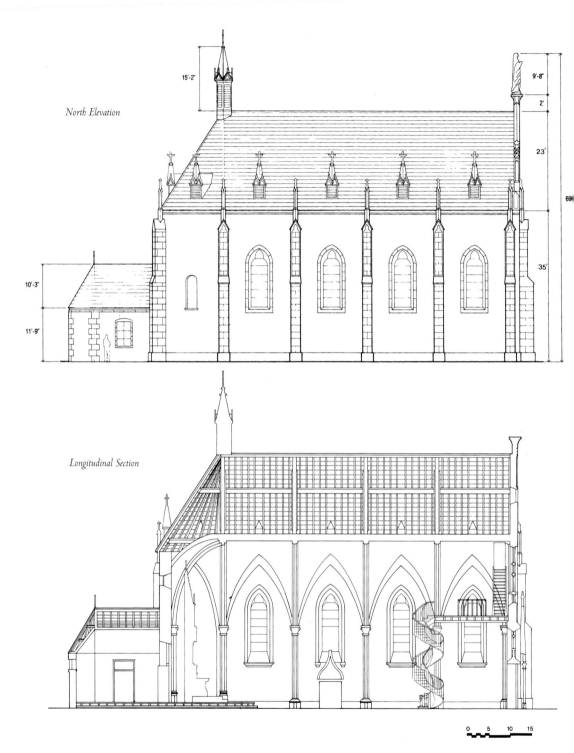

North Elevation

15'-2"

9'-8"

2'

23'

69'

35'

10'-3"

11'-9"

Longitudinal Section

0   5   10   15

80

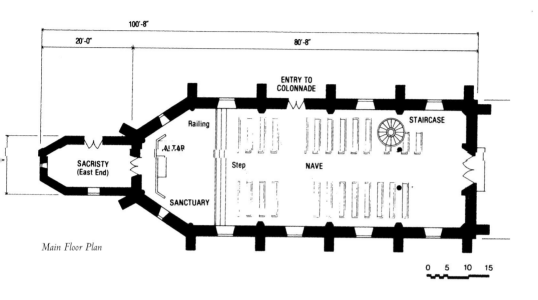

100'-8"

20'-0"

80'-8"

ENTRY TO
COLONNADE

Railing

STAIRCASE

ALTAR

SACRISTY
(East End)

Step

NAVE

SANCTUARY

Main Floor Plan

0   5   10   15

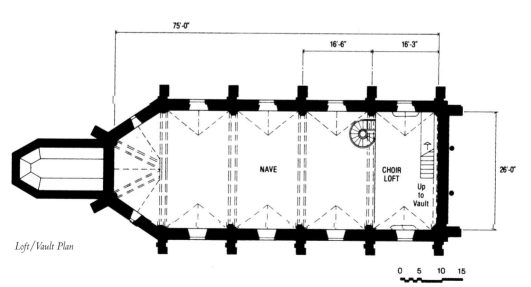

75'-0"

16'-6"

16'-3"

NAVE

CHOIR
LOFT

Up
to
Vault

26'-0"

Loft/Vault Plan

0   5   10   15

APPENDIX B

HARMONIUM

HARMONIUM STOPS

ALEXANDRE-FRANÇOIS DEBAIN
HARMONIUM
PARIS FRANCE, CA. 1867

(1) Sourdine (draws 1 via 3, 1 1/4" holes, to create a soft accompaniment stop)

(SP) Saxophone (draws tremblant on 1, draws 4 via a small adjustable port reduce air and cause wide celeste effect)

(10) Contre Basse (draws 2 and 6)

(5)(6) Dolce (8')

(0) Forte (opens a flap to louden 3, 4, 6)

(4)(4) Basson (8')

(3)(3) Clarion (4')

(2)(2) Bourdon (16')

(1)(1) Cor Anglais (8') small adjustable

(G) Grand Jeu (draws 1, 2, 3, 4, and treble 1, and 2, 3, 4)

Left knee lever draws G; expression knob (between levers); right knee lever draws 1/2

(1/2) Grand Jeu (draws treble only, 1, 2, 3, 4)

(1)(1) Flute (8')

(2)(2) Clarinette (16')

(3)(3) Fifre (4')

(4)(4) Hautbois (8')

(0) Forte (opens a flap to louden 3, 4, 5)

(5)(5) Musette (16')

(6) Celeste (16' and also draws 5)

(SP) Soprano (draws tremblant on 1, draws 4 via a small adjustabletable port to reduce air and wide celeste effect)

(T) Tremblant (works only on 1 via small valve)

Serial Number: (original) 17372 (number 2 somewhat obscured). Rebuilt, with Serial no. 18358 (about 1882/83) restruck over the original serial number.

Case: Flat-top, light golden oak, with two narrow, turned reeded columns on either side of the front, beneath the case ends. Width, 49 1/2"; height, 38 1/4"; depth, 26 1/2".
Compass: "C," 61 notes; bass, 29 notes, C to E, 1–29; treble, 32 notes, F to C, 32–61.

"Debain-Paris" is stamped above the bass Tremblant. Names penciled inside the reed pan: "Paris 1867 Edouard Ege; Répare par Edouard Ege—Juillet 1883; Repaired August Wehrle 1886; Repaired J. H. Thomas March 25, 1907, Denver Colo." "Lemire" is stamped on the outside of the reed pan with a pencil line through it and "Prepare De" written below. Below the Expression knob is an engraved brass plaque stating, "For Bishop Lamy, Santa Fe, New-Mexico." The Debain Harmonium is owned by the Archbishop of the Archdiocese of Santa Fe and is on loan to the Chapel of Our Lady of Light. It is housed in the choir gallery of the chapel.

In 1981 the harmonium was restored by the Roy Redman Organ Co., Fort Worth, Texas. Paper stopfaces for Bass and/or Treble 1, 2, 3, and 4 have the Bass and/or Treble clef sign with the staff and the notes of its range. A small "Ventola" blower was added during restoration.

Dr. James M. Bratton
Denver, Colorado

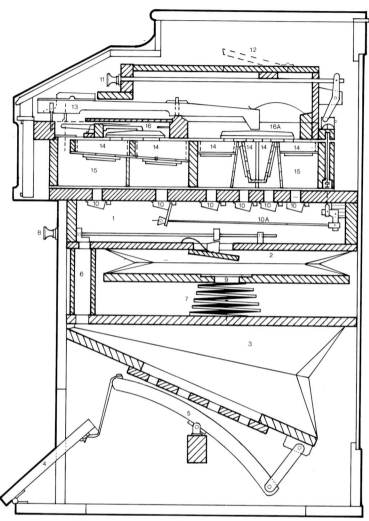

Dimensions: 38 $\frac{1}{4}$'h., 26 $\frac{1}{2}$'w., 49 $\frac{1}{2}$'d.

1	Windchest	7	Bellows Spring	12	Swell Forte
2	Reservoir	8	Expression	13	Key
3	Feeder	9	Exhaust Pallet	14	Reed Cells
4	Foot Treadle	10	Stop Valve	15	Reed Pan
5	Rocker	10A	Stop Action	16	Pallet of Front Organ
6	Wind-trunck or Chimney	11	Drawstop	16A	Pallet of Back Organ

APPENDIX C
STAIRCASE DRAWING

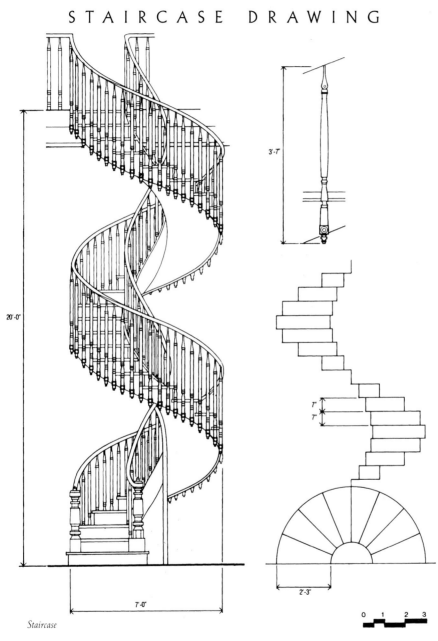

20'-0"

3'-7"

7"
7"

2'-3"

7'-0"

Staircase

0 1 2 3

NOTES

Chapter 1

THE SISTERS OF LORETTO AND HOW THEY GREW

1. *Daily New Mexican*, July 12, 1875.

2. Ibid., Oct. 30, 1876.

3. Ibid., June 11, 1877.

4. Segale, *Santa Fe Trail*, 158.

5. *Daily New Mexican*, Aug. 23, 1877.

6. Ibid., Nov. 17, 1877.

7. Santa Fe Annals (SFA) 1852, Loretto Motherhouse Archives (LMA). At the request of the U.S. Postmaster the spelling of Nerinckx was simplified to Nerinx.

8. Maes, *Nerinckx*, 76.

9. Wolff, *Generation to Generation*, 1–7.

10. Misc. Documents, Archives of the Archdiocese of Santa Fe (AASF), copy of Lamy letter to Purcell, Santa Fe, N.M., Sept. 2, 1851; original in Notre Dame Archives.

11. Read, *Illustrated History*, 98.

12. Warner, *Archbishop Lamy*, 280. *Atole*, a thin corn mush or gruel, was a staple of early New Mexico diet. Lamy and Vicar-General J. P. Machebeuf rode a pair of matched bay mules. See Howlett, *Machebeuf*, 216–17.

13. *Albuquerque Journal*, Dec. 27, 1982. Author-teacher Ray John de Aragón of Las Vegas, N.M., petitioned former Archbishop Robert F. Sánchez of the Archdiocese of Santa Fe to reinstate Padre Martínez into the Catholic Church. Scholar-poet Fray Angélico Chávez questioned whether Martínez was in fact canonically excommunicated by Lamy. See Chávez, *But Time and Chance*, for an analysis of the conflict and parochial nature of the padre's excommunication.

14. Horgan, *Lamy*, 117.

15. Ibid., 8–9.

16. McCann, "Archbishop Purcell," 46.

17. Misc. Documents, AASF. Emmitsburg is in Maryland.

18. SFA 1852, LMA.

19. Gregg, in Moorhead, ed., *Commerce*, 23 n. 2; Gregg, *Road to Santa Fe*, 1.

20. SFA 1852, LMA. Mother Matilda's tombstone in Woodlawn Cemetery, Independence, Mo., reads July 16 rather than July 17, 1852.

21. Ibid.

22. Mother Magdalen Hayden's practice Spanish letterbook, of MMH, LMA. As an exercise, Mother Magdalen translated letters to her friends and family from English into Spanish in a bound book. Fort Barclay, two miles north of Watrous, N.M., was a forage camp, not a government fort. Wagon trains on the Santa Fe Trail often stopped there for protection against Indian raids.

23. Drown, "Escorting a Bishop," 197–98; MMH, LMA.

24. MMH, LMA.

25. Gregg, in Moorhead, ed., *Commerce*, 77–80.

26. Laughlin, *The Wind Leaves No Shadow*, 317. The Santa Fe Trail is visible for several miles from Talaya Hill (also known as San Estevan).

27. MMH, LMA.

28. Ibid.

29. Segale, *Santa Fe Trail*, 97.

30. Russell in Brayer, ed., *Land of Enchantment*, 51.

31. Libro de Caja, 27 de Setiembre 1852 and Day book no. 6, Julio de 1873, LMA;

partido contract between Pablo Moya and Madre del Convento de Nuestra Señora de la Luz, 31 de Marzo de 1867, LMA. A *partido* was a livestock contract. See Parish, *Ilfeld Company*, 150–73.

32. SFA 1853, LMA.

33. *Santa Fe Weekly Gazette*, Oct. 7, 1865.

34. MMH, LMA.

35. Russell in Brayer, ed., *Land of Enchantment*, 42–43. Marian Russell erroneously recalled the spiral staircase in St. Francis Cathedral rather than in the Chapel of Our Lady of Light.

36. MMH, LMA.

37. Ibid.

38. SFA 1854, LMA.

39. MMH, LMA.

40. SFA 1854, LMA.

41. Contract of sale, July 29, 1857, LMA.

42. MMH, LMA.

43. Davis, *El Gringo*, 166. Mother Magdalen wrote that "our house consists of fifteen rooms." Paul Horgan cites an 1852 letter of Lamy's Vicar-General Machebeuf to his sister as indicating the year of purchase of a "26-room house" costing sixty-five hundred *piastres* (a *piastre* was the equivalent of a peso). The exact number of rooms is unclear. Deed Book B, Santa Fe County Records, shows that Preston Beck sold the Casa Americana to Lamy on Aug. 15, 1854, and deeded it to him on Dec. 29, 1856.

44. Santa Fe Deed File, LMA. San Miguel, known earlier as San Miguel del Bado, was an important way-stop and river crossing on the Santa Fe Trail between Santa Fe and Las Vegas, N.M.

45. MMH, LMA.

46. Ibid. According to the Instrument of Indenture recorded in Deed Book C, Santa Fe County Records, the cost of the Jackson property was $1,500 not $1,000, as noted by Mother Magdalen.

47. Chronology of property purchased by the Sisters of Loretto:

July 29, 1857   Casa Americana and land purchased from Lamy for $3,000, deeded Feb. 3, 1859.

October 21, 1859   House and lot to north purchased from Manuel Antonio Sandoval for $500.

November 1, 1859   House and lot to north and west of Sandoval property purchased from Territorial Secretary Alexander M. Jackson for $1,500.

November 10, 1859   Lot to north purchased from Estate of Dámaso López for $500.

February 8, 1861   Property purchased from María del Carmen Ávila for $800.

December 4, 1862   Property purchased from José Manuel Archuleta for $550.

February 11, 1863   Property purchased from Estate of G. H. Estes for $200.

Santa Fe Deed File, LMA; MMH, LMA; Deed Books B and C, Santa Fe County Records.

Chapter 2

TIMES OF TROUBLE, TIMES OF JOY

1. MMH, LMA. See F. S. Donnell, "When Las Vegas Was the Capital of New Mexico," 265–72.

2. MMH, LMA.

3. Ibid.

4. Alberts, *Rebels*, 91.

5. Act of Incorporation (copy), Jan. 5, 1874, LMA. Original document lost.

6. *Daily New Mexican*, Oct. 18, 1869. The erroneous date of July 24, 1869, for the laying of the St. Francis Cathedral cornerstone has been perpetuated since Defouri's *Historical Sketch of the Catholic Church in New Mexico*.

7. Chávez, *Cathedral*, 24–32; Twitchell, *Old Santa Fe*, 364–65. The author climbed Cerro Colorado, which is privately owned, in Oct. 1982. The original Cerro

Mogino has been demolished, as well as the adjacent volcanic hills to the north.

8. Segale, *Santa Fe Trail*, 132–33. Perhaps Sister Blandina referred to the lack of a staircase to the choir loft.

9. Ibid., 113, 121, 178, 182–83.

10. Ibid., 155.

11. Ibid., 94, 121, 183; *New Mexican*, Nov. 22, 1879. Projectus (Priest, his Christian name) Mouly was born Feb. 15, 1851, to Antoine Mouly and Catherine Retail of Volvic, France. Naissances de Volvic 1843–1852, Archives of the Department of Puy-de-Dôme. No Mouly chapel drawings have been found. The stained-glass windows in L'eglise Saint-Priest (Volvic) were made by the same firm in Clermont-Ferrand as those in Loretto Chapel. Mrs. Guillaume Coulloudon referred to Mouly in her letters to her husband as that "boy who has no family or responsibilities and keeps you away from your family." It is curious that Mouly's funeral was held in St. Vincent Hospital rather than Loretto Chapel, the building which "remains a monument to his professional skill and ability," according to the local newspaper.

12. SFA 1880, LMA.

13. Day book no. 6, LMA.

14. *Daily New Mexican*, Jan. 7, 1881. The firm of Monier & Coulloudon met with financial ruin after the construction of the Santa Fe Water Works in the 1890s, according to Mariette Coulloudon Cunico.

15. *Portrait and Biographical Record of Arizona*, 852–53; *Arizona Daily Star*, Oct. 18, 1923. The list of Tucson buildings constructed by Quintus Monier (1855–1923), owner of the Tucson Pressed Brick Company, is substantial. Along with numerous private residences, schools, railroad roundhouses, and commercial structures, he constructed a boys' dormitory, a science building, and an agriculture building at the University of Arizona. Monier also did construction work in Phoenix, Douglas, Bisbee, Yuma, and Nogales.

16. Interview with Mariette Coulloudon Cunico, July 23, 1983. Mrs. Cunico owns a collection of letters written by her grandfather, François-Guillaume

(William) Coulloudon, to his wife, Mariette Courtial Coulloudon, in Paris, France, dating from 1874.

17. Ibid. William Coulloudon mentioned the following names of fellow workmen in his letters: John Desfarges (stonemason), a Messr. Blanchot (called a *roullabat*, or one who does the hauling to the scaffolds, from Issoire, Auvergne), a Messr. Durant, a Messr. Monier (Coulloudon's partner, whose given name appears on the 1880 U.S. Census for Santa Fe as Cassian but appears as "Q" Monier on the sisters' books), Michael Digneo (stonemason), and Etienne Lacassagne (carpenter and plasterer), also mentioned in Sister Blandina Segale's *Santa Fe Trail*, 136. Coulloudon wrote that the cathedral was a "monstrous" project which was to resume after the completion of the chapel. He uses the word *piastre* when referring to money (roughly the equivalent of one peso).

18. Giomi, "Italian Pioneers," 12–16.

19. Segale, *Santa Fe Trail*, 134. Architects Antoine and Projectus Mouly were from the village of Volvic, near Clermont-Ferrand, Puy-de-Dôme, France. The family of Lamy's close friend the Rev. Joseph P. Machebeuf were also from Volvic.

20. Ibid.

21. *New Mexican*, Sept. 13, 1879. The nephew of Archbishop Lamy usually signed his name "J. B. Lamy" and was also called "John B. Lamy." However, during the murder trial and subsequent divorce proceedings (later dismissed) between J. B. Lamy and his wife, Mercedes Cháves, the title of "Jr." was added to his name. No doubt this was to avoid any confusion with the archbishop, who had the same name.

22. U.S. Census Records, Santa Fe County, 1870, 1880.

23. Will of Sister Stanislaus Cháves, LMA.

24. SFA 1878, LMA.

25. Ibid., 1881.

26. Ibid., 1878.

27. Bloom, "Bourke on the Southwest," 318–19.

28. SFA 1878, LMA.

29. Photo from E. Boyd Collection, NMSA.

30. SFA 1887, LMA; interview with Sr. Florence Wolff, Archivist, LMA, Jan. 10, 1983.

31. Segale, *Santa Fe Trail*, 168; *Revista Católica*, 19 de Febrero de 1888; Horgan, *Lamy*, 440.

32. MMH, LMA.

33. The academy building was originally a three-story adobe structure. Architect John Gaw Meem removed the third story because of its instability. In 1939 the stable, milk shed, and chicken houses on the southeast corner of the sisters' property were converted into the Opportunity School for challenged children.

34. *Daily New Mexican*, Mar. 6, 1881; Sept. 15, 1892.

35. Barbour, *Yucca Land*, 43.

36. SFA 1880, LMA. The sisters traveled on the Denver & Rio Grande Railroad known as the Chili Line. It was the first narrow-gauge track in the U.S. projected as a north-south trunk line connecting Denver and Mexico City. The tracks were taken up during World War II.

37. SFA 1908, LMA.

38. Ibid. Photo confirms window above altar opened earlier than 1908.

39. Ibid.

40. Ibid. Statement from J. Daniel, Paris, France, 1887, LMA; SFA 1888–89, LMA.

41. MMH, LMA.

Chapter 3

THE CHAPEL AS ARCHITECTURE

1. Interview with Sr. Florence Wolff, Loretto Motherhouse Archivist, Sept. 1, 1983. It seems to be more a matter of tradition than actual written history that the sisters compared their Chapel of Our Lady of Light to the Sainte-Chapelle.

2. Christopher, Conron, Krasin, Moul, and Weismantel, *Design & Preservation*, 18–19.

3. Hafen, *Ruxton of the Rockies*, 180.

4. Gregg, in Moorhead, ed., *Commerce*, 144. *Palacio* meaning the Palace of the Governors.

5. Grodecki, *Sainte-Chapelle*, 29. The church architecture of Basse-Auvergne, place of origin of many of the French workers who built Loretto Chapel, is Romanesque.

6. Warner, *Archbishop Lamy*, 173.

7. Richter, "Sister Mallon's Journal," 143; SFA 1880, LMA.

8. Bunting, *Early Architecture*, 102.

9. Twitchell, *Leading Facts*, 13 n. 373.

10. Adams and Chávez, *Missions*, 32, 37. The Chapel of Our Lady of Light built by the Sisters of Loretto was not the first chapel by that name to have existed in Santa Fe. Don Francisco Marin del Valle, governor, constructed a chapel in 1760 at his own expense on the south side of the plaza opposite the Palace of the Governors. An historic plaque now marks the site on the wall of a present-day building. La Castrense, also called the Chapel of Our Lady of Light, was a military chapel used for worship by Spanish soldiers. Its exquisitely carved *reredos* may be seen today in the Cristo Rey Church in Santa Fe, installed in 1940. Originally from La Castrense and later incorporated into the reredos, the stone medallion of Our Lady of Light in bas-relief was given to the sisters by Bishop Lamy around 1853 before the trade of the chapel to Simón Delgado in 1859. The carving remained embedded in the adobe wall near the entrance to the sisters' old convent until 1892. The close association of Lamy and the sisters, plus the fact that Santa Fe had a chapel by that name, substantially influenced the naming of the convent and chapel after Our Lady of Light. Over the years, the Convent and Academy of Our Lady of Light became known simply as "Loretto," the how and why unclear even to the sisters themselves. In 1970 the Historic Santa Fe Foundation plaqued it as "Our Lady of Light Loretto Chapel." For an in-depth study of La Castrense, see Stubbs and Ellis, *Archaeological Investigations*.

11. Warner, *Archbishop Lamy*, 173; Kubler, *Religious Architecture*, 141; Wilson, "Architecture Transformations," 9.

12. Kessell, *Missions*, 18.

13. Grodecki, *Sainte-Chapelle*, 18.

14. Viollet-le-Duc, *Discourses*, 281, 466, 483.

15. Ibid.

16. Kessell, *Missions*, 19.

17. The Our Lady of Lourdes statues are very similar. The statue of Loretto Chapel was blessed in 1888, the same year the statue at San Juan was erected.

18. Wilson, "Architecture Transformations," 9. Chris Wilson also compares the Chapel of Our Lady of Light to the church at Galisteo, N.M., which he calls a "fascinating descendant." The gable he mentions, however, has been altered.

19. An architectural study on the chapel is not yet accomplished.

20. The original wooden finials have been replaced with metal.

21. Viollet-le-Duc, *Discourses*, 483.

22. See note 27 in Chapter 2 regarding Bourke's account of the chapel in 1881.

23. Coulloudon to his wife, Oct. 22, 1877.

24. Ibid.

25. Scobey, *Stained Glass*, 22–23.

26. Rabaud, *Sainte-Chapelle*, 29; Loriaux letter, Feb. 24, 1977.

27. Scobey, *Stained Glass*, 23.

28. Webber, *Symbolism*, 92.

29. It is worth noting that the firm of J. Daniel, Paris, France, submitted to the Sisters of Loretto an elaborate drawing of a proposed altar for the chapel, dated June 1, 1887, which was not purchased. The statue of Our Lady of Lourdes was purchased from the same firm that same year.

30. Viollet-le-Duc states that until very late, architects held the title of master-mason as well. The graves of architects Projectus Mouly and François Mallet are unmarked. The cemetery office has no burial plat of early graves. Mother Magdalen Hayden is also buried there.

Chapter 4

THE MYSTERIOUS SPIRAL STAIRCASE

1. Manion, "Santa Fe's Spiral Staircase," 22–25.

2. *Santa Fe New Mexican*, Oct. 26, 1914. Interview with Virginia Koplin Stauffer.

3. Unidentified Riverbank, Calif., newspaper clipping, Hesch Family Files. The Hesch name does not appear on the 1880 U.S. Census for Santa Fe County; however, the name of Philip [*sic*] Hesch does appear on the Titusville, Pa., 1880 U.S. Census, where he lived before moving to Santa Fe. His name is spelled "Phillip" in the Hesch family Bible.

4. *New Mexican*, April 29, 30, 1946.

5. Diaries of Lt. John G. Bourke, 1243–1244, USMA.

6. Day book no. 9, Feb. 1886 to Sept. 1896, LMA.

7. *Daily New Mexican*, Nov. 8, 1887.

8. Grace Family History.

9. Interview with Rudy Yardman (grandson of Charles Frederick Yardman); Notice to Thieves, Thugs, Fakirs and Bunko Steerers, Misc. Records, Wanted Persons no. 11, NMSA; obit, *New Mexican*, April 10, 1910. A bunko steerer is one who engages in a swindling scheme or game.

10. *New Mexican*, Feb. 26, 1970. The family spelling of the elder Hadwiger was "Yohon" rather than "Johann."

11. *Pueblo Chieftain*, Feb. 22, 1976. See Kaplan, "Solving a 100-Year-Old Mystery," 14–19; Cehanowicz, "Oscar Hadwiger and the Miraculous Staircase"; and "Two Members Claim to Have Solved the Riddle of the Miraculous Stairway."

12. Sister Ludavine Mueller to O. E. Hadwiger, Oct. 5, 196, LMA.

13. Sister Ludavine Mueller to Mr. and Mrs. Hadwiger, undated, LMA.

14. In November 1938 the staircase, including its legend, was entered in a Ripley contest in the *Denver Post* by Angeline A. Guerin of Las Vegas, N.M. Ripley Archives.

15. In 1886 Monier is listed as one of the capitol stone contractors; he did repairs on the Palace of the Governors and also held the contract for the Santa Fe Water Works, built in the 1890s. *New Mexican*, July 9, 1886.

16. *Santa Fe New Mexican*, Jan. 5, 1895. The sanitarium, built by the Sisters of Charity, burned down in June 1896. The building was immediately north of St. Francis Cathedral. Quintus Monier, descendant of several generations of stonemasons, was born Oct. 23, 1853, in Aigueperse, Puy-de-Dôme, France.

17. See Harris, "I owe them a lot; they taught me the love of work," 98–106, 109–80; Truant, *The Rites of Labor*; and Icher, *Les Compagnons*.

18. The Willi and Flora Spiegelberg house on Palace Avenue in Santa Fe, which has a French mansard roof, was built in 1880. The author believes that Quintus Monier assisted in its construction; Monier was a partner of Spiegelberg in at least one business venture.

19. Since 1996 the author has been a guest several times of Dr. Jean-Pierre Marliac in Aigueperse, Puy-de-Dôme. This is the village where the Monier family lived. Vicar-General Eguillon came from this area as well. Michel Allaeys, an architect cousin of Quintus Monier from Aigueperse, assisted in searching for family letters which Monier might have written to France describing the building of the spiral staircase. None has been found to date. Librarian Marie-Claude Boismenu of Volvic wrote an article about the Volvic-Santa Fe connection for a Riom newspaper in 1979.

20. The newspaper item naming Rochas as the staircase builder was inadvertently missed by earlier researchers. The author found the name of Rochas in one of the sisters' accounting books during research in 1984 at the Loretto Motherhouse in Nerinx, Kentucky. Because Rochas was recorded as working on a building other than the chapel, his name was not included in the list of possible staircase carpenters at the time.

21. Day book no. 8, Marzo de 1881, 89, LMA. The academy building was three stories high, which would have required several conventional staircases. The following advertisement appears in the June 17, 1881, *Daily New Mexican:* "Stair Building and other job work done at the carpenter shop near the small foot bridge. Orders left with Dr. Sargent will receive prompt attention." In an 1881 photo by Ben Wittick taken from the Don Gaspar Street area, the sign of a carpenter's shop across Old Santa Fe Trail from the chapel is visible.

22. The author attempted to trace freight records, but none could be found; the railroad arrived in New Mexico eight months prior to Rochas. Measurements for the staircase height required the completion of the choir loft. Had the shipping of the heavy staircase pieces been delayed between 1878 and 1880, awaiting the arrival of the railroad in New Mexico? Telephone interview by the author in Grenoble, France, with Daniel Patoux, of Valbelle, France. Patoux, editor of *Les Compagnons*, newsletter of the centuries-old craft guild of France, said it would not have been unusual for Rochas to have built the spiral staircase gratis had he been a compagnon. These highly skilled men were the stonecutters and carpenters who built France's great cathedrals and chateaux. They possessed the love of manual work, or *la belle ouvrage*; they exist today. However, it cannot be documented that François-Jean Rochas was indeed a member of this group, which requires a lengthy apprenticeship of many years.

23. Dog Canyon, a few miles south of Alamogordo, N.M., is today part of the Oliver Lee Memorial State Park. The park is open to the public. There is a small museum, and outside are the partially restored remains of the rock cabin built by Frank Rochas. For a discussion of Billy the Kid and the Lincoln County War, see Frederick Nolan, *The Lincoln County War*.

24. Author C. L. Sonnichsen read the manuscript for the first edition of *Loretto: The Sisters and Their Santa Fe Chapel*, published in 1984. Though Sonnichsen's book, *Tularosa* (Albuquerque, rev. 1980), included an entire chapter on Frank Rochas, entitled "The Bravest Man in New Mexico," the link of Rochas to northern New Mexico and the spiral staircase with that of Rochas's 1894 unmailed letter from Dog Canyon to Q. Monier in Santa Fe escaped detection. Dr. Sonnichsen died before the author made the discovery.

25. Estate of Frank Rochas 1895, Doña Ana County Probate Records, Las Cruces, N.M. I am indebted to Peter L. Eidenbach and Human Systems Research, Inc., Tularosa, N.M., for the thorough research in New Mexico and France accomplished at the time the Oliver Lee Memorial State Park at Dog Canyon was planned in 1979. The one-room rock cabin built by Frank Rochas has since been

restored. Artifacts found in the cabin ruins are presently on exhibit in the park museum.

26. In 1995 the author visited Vif, France, where she interviewed distant members of the Rochas family. As established during the 1979 research for the park at Dog Canyon in southern N.M., the Rochas family knows very little about the life and talent of Frank Rochas. It seems that someone in France had prior knowledge of the carpentry ability of François-Jean Rochas. Yet, any carpentry done by Rochas in or near Vif, before he immigrated to the United States, is yet to be found.

27. See Chapter 2 for the earliest staircase description (April 1881) by Lt. John G. Bourke. The author has found a laboratory in Paris that can analyze a small wood sample from the staircase and give an informed opinion regarding the wood species, whether it is from France or the U.S. This might solve the dilemma. Understandably, to date the chapel owner has been reluctant to remove any sample from the staircase stringer (and tread) in the fear that its removal might jeopardize the staircase integrity.

28. New York Passenger Lists, Aug. 27–Sept. 25, 1880, film no. 0295794, LDS. The name of Rochas appears at the end of the *St. Laurent* manifest, followed by the number 5157. It is listed among several other names enumerated as "Agents." While there is no given name or age for Rochas, it is reasonable to assume that this is indeed carpenter François-Jean. The number probably indicates he is the agent for some freight, perhaps his carpenter's tools and the cut staircase. The 1870 U.S. Census for Paraje, Socorro County, N.M., shows a young French clerk working for Numa Reymond. Additionally, the 1880 census indicates that two Swiss clerks were employed. Reymond apparently brought immigrant Europeans to work for him in his Paraje merchandising store; by 1880 the railroad had bypassed Paraje for San Marcial, and he then moved to Las Cruces.

29. Doña Ana County Clerk Records.

30. *The Sun*, Socorro, N.M., June 10, 1883, describes the Sisters of Loretto and "marked additions" to their building of a second story, which was nearing com-

pletion. It is possible that Rochas and Monier arrived together in Socorro in late 1882 or early 1883 to assist the sisters in their construction.

31. Price, *Mesilla Valley Pioneers*, 185. Today, Dog Canyon is part of the Oliver Lee Memorial State Park, south of Alamogordo, N.M.

32. Coulloudon Letters, Mariette Coulloudon Cunico.

33. The Rochas estate inventory included 3 lots of tools: 2 hammers, 4 saws, 2 try squares, 1 saw clamp, 1 bench anvil, 9 planes, 1 glue pot, 19 molding planes, 1 dring (draw) knife, 3 augers, 1 brace, 10 auger bits, 1 reamer, 2 screwdrivers, 1 pair Trammel points (used for drawing large circles), 1 steel square, 1 saw large (broken), 1 saw miter (broken), 5 gauges (?), 6 chisels, 2 gouges, 1 saw set, and 2 clamps. Doña Ana County Probate Records.

34. The name appears as John H. Morris (Morrison added below Morris), Breckenridge, Texas. Record of Convicts, New Mexico Penitentiary, Convict Record Books 1884–1917, roll 1, NMSA.

35. Ibid.

36. The burial entry of François-Jean Rochas could not be found in the Catholic Church records. At the time of Rochas's death, apparently no priest was available in the remote village of La Luz, N.M., a small community near Dog Canyon that had no full-time priest.

Chapter 5

THE HARMONIUM

1. Marcuse, *Instruments*, 228.

2. Patent and title description taken from plaque above keyboard of harmonium.

3. *New Grove Dictionary*, 169.

4. *Musical Instruments of the World*, 14.

5. Marcuse, *Instruments*, 229.

6. Smithsonian Institution, *Checklist*, 72. The Musée Instrumental du Conservatoire Royal de Musique, Brussels, Belgium, collection contains three Debain instruments acquired after publication of their catalog, according to Malou Haines of Brussels, Belgium.

7. *Bourgeois Gentilhomme*, with elaborate explanatory essay on the use of the harmonium; *Salome, Feuersnot*, by Richard Strauss; *Bagatelles* for two violins, cello, and harmonium, op. 47, by Dvoràk; a version of Busoni's *Berceuse élégiaque* adapted for harmonium; two waltzes by Johann Strauss adapted for harmonium and string quartet (performed by Alban Berg); *Five Orchestral Pieces*, op. 16, adapted for chamber orchestra with harmonium (Felix Greissle, 1925), by Schoenberg; and *Kunst des Registrierens für Harmonium* (Berlin, 1911–14), by Karg-Elert.

8. MMH, LMA.

9. Father Charles Nerinckx brought a chamber organ to the U.S. in 1817, said to be the first organ in Kentucky. See Maes, *Nerinckx*, 355. This organ may be found at the Loretto Motherhouse in Nerinx, Kentucky.

10. Libro de Caja, 27 de Setiembre de 1852, LMA.

11. Day book no. 6, 1866–1876, LMA.

12. Letter written in Spanish, Loretto Sister Stanislaus Chávez to Archbishop Lamy in Paris, Agosto 26 de 185 (incomplete year date), Santa Fe, asking him to purchase a hearing aid for her. Author's collection.

13. From an engraving of the atelier of Alexandre-François Debain by Simon, courtesy of Malou Haines, Brussels, Belgium.

14. The railroad did not reach Lamy, N.M., seventeen miles south of Santa Fe, until 1880.

15. Loose Documents 1850–1851, AASF.

16. Apel, *Harvard Dictionary*, 256; Horgan, *Lamy*, 122; Gregg, *Road to Santa Fe*, 134. A *fandango* as a musical composition is an eighteenth-century dance of moderate-to-quick rhythm with sung couplets. In New Mexico it described a dance party, or *baile*.

17. Sunder, *Matt Field*, 253.

18. Abert, *Report of Lieut. J. W. Abert*, 417–548.

19. Drumm, *Down the Santa Fe Trail*, 138.

20. Horgan, *Lamy*, 331.

21. Ibid., 339.

22. *Revista Católica*, 7 de Abril de 1877.

23. Memoirs of Sister Bernard Doyle, Mar. 1938, LMA.

24. Interview of Sister Florence Wolff, with Sister Orline Tefler, Denver, Colo., Mar. 1983, LMA.

25. The name of August Wehrle appears in the *Daily Colorado Chieftain*, Pueblo, Colo., Jan. 30, 1877, as an itinerant "tuner and repairer of pianos and organs" from Denver.

26. SFA 1945, LMA; photo of Hammond organ being raised to choir loft, LMA. Upon discovery of the Debain harmonium in 1975, the author found a large hole opened into the rear of the instrument, indicating that the sisters had at some time in the past employed a blower to assist the player. The hand-operated blower was later found abandoned in the vault area over the chapel.

27. *New Mexican*, Feb. 21, 1971.

28. Dedication program, July 4, 1982; the author performed the Dvorák five *Bagatelles*, op. 47.

GLOSSARY

acequia	irrigation ditch
adobe	mud, a mud brick
adz	cutting tool having an arching blade set at right angles to the handle
apse	circular or multiangular termination of a church sanctuary
Arroyo Saiz	small stream or gutter on East Palace Avenue at Delgado Street
baluster	upright support in the railing of a staircase
Cerro Colorado	red hill, near Lamy, N.M.
Cerro Mogino	hill west of Santa Fe, since demolished for volcanic tuft
ciénega	marsh, area of springs
crocket	projecting block or spur of stone to decorate raking lines formed by angles

diocese	province over which a bishop has authority
finial	upper portion of a pinnacle or other architectural feature
flèche	arrow, term applied to a slender wooden spire rising from a roof
fresco	fresh; term applied to painting on a wall while the plaster is wet
in partibus infidelium	in the regions of unbelievers
La Castrense	military chapel
latilla	small peeled pole used in ceilings
newel	post into which the handrail of a staircase is framed
oratory	private chapel
pallium	stole worn around the neck by an archbishop, a symbol of office
parroquia	parish church as distinguished from a mission
partido	share, livestock contract akin to sharecropping of the South
pilaster	pillar engaged in a wall, from which its capital and base project
pintle	pivot pin of a hinge

plaza	public square
reredos	screen behind an altar
strap hinge	hinge that projects beyond the back stile of a door and fits over the vertical pintle
tablas	short adzed boards used in ceilings
Te Deum	ancient Latin hymn of praise to God
territorial style	architectural style of flat roof with brick coping brought to Santa Fe in the mid-nineteenth century
trèfoil	three leaves; term applied to this distribution in Gothic tracery
vicariate	jurisdiction of a vicar

BIBLIOGRAPHY

Archival Collections

Archives of the Archdiocese of Santa Fe.

    Loose Documents 1850–1851.

    Misc. Documents.

Archives of the Department of Puy-de-Dôme, Clermont-Ferrand, France.

    Naissances de Volvic 1843–1852.

Church of Jesus Christ of Latter-day Saints, Salt Lake City, Utah.

    New York Passenger Lists, August 27–September 25, 1880.

Grace Family History, Santa Fe.

Loretto Motherhouse Archives, Nerinx, Kentucky.

    Act of Incorporation (copy), January 5, 1874.

    Bernard M. Burns, Archdiocese of Santa Fe, to Sister Antonella, Santa Fe, New Mexico, August 10, 1938.

    Contract of sale, July 29, 1857.

    Day book no. 6, January 1867 to May 1879.

    Day book no. 8, Marzo de 1881.

    Day book no. 9, February 1886 to September 1896.

    Interview of Sister Florence Wolff with Sister Orline Tefler, Denver, Colorado, March 1983.

    Libro de Caja, 27 de Setiembre 1852.

    Ludavine Mueller, Superior, to O. E. Hadwiger, Santa Fe, New Mexico, October 5, 1965.

Memoirs of Sister Bernard Doyle, March 1938.

Mother Magdalen Hayden practice Spanish letterbook.

Partido contract, 31 de Marzo de 1867.

Santa Fe Annals, 1852–1854, 1878, 1880, 1887–1889, 1908.

Santa Fe Deed File.

Statement from J. Daniel, Paris, France, 1887.

New Mexico State Archives, Santa Fe.

Misc. Records, Wanted Persons.

New Mexico Penitentiary, convict record books 1884–1917.

Ripley Archives, Toronto, Canada.

U.S. Military Academy Library, West Point, New York.

Diaries of Lt. John G. Bourke, U.S. Army, Vol. 39 (April 18, 1881).

Interviews

Mariette Coulloudon Cunico, July 10, 23, 1983. Albuquerque, New Mexico.

Daniel Patoux, Sept. 18, 1996, Sept. 20, 1998, and Oct. 2, 2000. Valbelle, Ardêche, France, and Paris, France.

Virginia Koplin Stauffer, August 15, 1983. Santa Fe, New Mexico.

Sr. Florence Wolff, September 7, 1983. Loretto Motherhouse, Nerinx, Kentucky.

Rudy Yardman, October 8, 1990. Santa Fe, New Mexico.

Newspapers

Albuquerque Journal

Arizona Daily Star, Tucson

Daily Colorado Chieftain, Pueblo

Denver Post

Pueblo Chieftain

Revista Católica, Las Vegas, New Mexico

Santa Fe New Mexican (and various names)

Santa Fe Weekly Gazette

The Sun, Socorro, New Mexico

Unpublished Sources

Chávez, Sister Stanislaus to Archbishop Lamy in Paris, Agosto 26 de 185-. Author's collection.

Coulloudon, François-Guillaume, letters. Mariette Coulloudon Cunico, Albuquerque, New Mexico.

Doña Ana County Clerk Records. Las Cruces, New Mexico.

Doña Ana County Probate Records.

Grace Family History. Santa Fe, New Mexico.

Hesch Family Files. Torrance, California.

Loriaux, Maurice, letter to Historic Santa Fe Foundation.

McCann, Sister Mary Agnes. "Archbishop Purcell and the Archdiocese of Cincinnati." Unpublished doctoral dissertation (1918), Catholic University of America.

Santa Fe County Records, Deed Books B and C.

Wilson, Chris. "Architecture Transformations: New Mexican Churches, 1351 to the Present." Unpublished manuscript (1979), University of New Mexico.

Published Sources

Abert, J. W. *Report of Lieut. J. W. Abert of His Examination of New Mexico, in the Years 1846–1847*, 30th Cong., 1st sess., House Exec. Doc. No. 41 (Serial 517). Washington, D.C.: Wendell and Van Benthuysen, 1848.

Adams, Eleanor B., and Fray Angélico Chávez. *The Missions of New Mexico, 1776: A Description by Fray Francisco Dominguez*. Albuquerque: University of New Mexico Press, 1975.

Alberts, Don E., ed. *Rebels on the Rio Grande: The Civil War Journal of A. B. Peticolas*. Albuquerque: University of New Mexico Press, 1984.

Apel, Willi. *Harvard Dictionary of Music*. Cambridge, Mass.: Harvard University Press, 1965.

Barbour, Sister Richard Marie, S.L. *Light in Yucca Land*. Santa Fe, N.M.: Shifani Brothers Printing Company, 1952.

Bloom, Lansing B. "Bourke on the Southwest." *New Mexico Historical Review* 10, no. 4 (October 1935).

Brayer, Garnet M., ed. *Land of Enchantment: Memoirs of Marian Russell along the Santa Fe Trail*. Evanston, Ill.: Branding Iron Press, 1954.

Bunting, Bainbridge. *Early Architecture in New Mexico*. Albuquerque: University of New Mexico Press, 1976.

Cather, Willa. *Death Comes for the Archbishop*. New York: Alfred A. Knopf, 1964.

Cehanowicz, Laura. "Oscar Hadwiger and the Miraculous Staircase." *Fine Woodworking* (May/June 1979).

Chávez, Fray Angélico. *But Time and Chance: The Story of Padre Martínez of Taos, 1793–1867*. Santa Fe, N.M.: Sunstone Press, 1981.

————. *The Santa Fe Cathedral of St. Francis of Assisi*. Santa Fe, N.M.: Shifani Brothers Printing, rev. 1978.

Christopher, R. Patrick, John P. Conron, Karalyn Krasin, Harry Moul, and William Weismantel. *Design & Preservation in Santa Fe: A Pluralistic Approach*. Santa Fe, N.M.: Planning Dept., City of Santa Fe, 1977.

Davis, W. W. H. *El Gringo: New Mexico and Her People*. Lincoln: University of Nebraska Press, 1982.

Defouri, Rev. James H. *Historical Sketch of the Catholic Church in New Mexico*. San Francisco: n.p., 1887.

Donnell, F. S. "When Las Vegas Was the Capital of New Mexico." *New Mexico Historical Review* 8, no. 4 (October 1933).

Drown, William. "Escorting a Bishop." *Everglade to Cañon* by Theo. F. Rodenbough. New York: D. Van Nostrand, 1875.

Drumm, Stella M., ed. *Down the Santa Fe Trail and into Mexico: The Diary of Susan Shelby Magoffin, 1846–1847*. Santa Fe, N.M.: William Gannon, 1975.

Florian, Sister M.O.S.F. "The Inexplicable Stairs." Reprint from *St. Joseph Magazine* (April 1960).

Giomi, Ioli, ed. "The Italian Pioneers in New Mexico from Santa Fe." *Il Giornalino* 4, no. 12 (January 1978).

Gregg, Kate L., ed. *The Road to Santa Fe: The Journal and Diaries of George Champlin Sibley*. Albuquerque: University of New Mexico Press, 1952.

Grodecki, Louis. *Sainte-Chapelle*. Paris: Caisse Nationale des Monuments Historiques (Editions et Documents), n.d.

Hafen, LeRoy B., ed. *Ruxton of the Rockies*. Norman: University of Oklahoma Press, 1979.

Harris, Joseph. "I owe them a lot; they taught me the love of work." *Smithsonian* 27, no. 3 (June 1996).

Horgan, Paul. *Lamy of Santa Fe: His Life and Times*. New York: Farrar, Straus and Giroux, 1975.

Howlett, Rev. W. J. *Life of the Right Reverend Joseph P. Machebeuf*. Pueblo, Colo.: n.p., 1908.

Icher, François. *Les Compagnons on l'amour de la belle ouvrage*. Découvertes Gallimard, n.d.

Kaplan, Howard M. "Solving a 100-Year-Old Mystery." Empire Magazine, *Denver Post*, August 15, 1976.

Kessell, John L. *The Missions of New Mexico Since 1776*. Albuquerque: University of New Mexico Press, 1980.

Kubler, George. *The Religious Architecture of New Mexico in the Colonial Period and Since the American Occupation*. Albuquerque: University of New Mexico Press, 1940.

Laughlin, Ruth. *The Wind Leaves No Shadow*. Caldwell, Idaho: Caxton Printers, Ltd., 1956.

Maes, Rev. Camillus P. *The Life of Rev. Charles Nerinckx: With a Chapter on the Early Catholic Missions of Kentucky.* Cincinnati, Ohio: Robert Clarke & Co., 1880.

Manion, Patricia Jean, S.L. "Santa Fe's Spiral Staircase." *Loretto* (Fall 1965).

Marcuse, Sibyl. *Musical Instruments: A Comprehensive Dictionary.* New York: W. W. Norton & Co., 1975.

Moorhead, Max L., ed. *Commerce of the Prairies.* Norman: University of Oklahoma Press, 1954.

Musical Instruments of the World. United States: Paddington Press, The Two Continents Publishing Group, 1976.

New Grove Dictionary of Music and Musicians. Vol. 8. London: Macmillan Publishers, Limited, 1980.

Nolan, Frederick. *The Lincoln County War: A Documentary History.* Norman: University of Oklahoma Press, 1992.

Parish, William J. *The Charles Ilfeld Company.* Cambridge: Harvard University Press, 1961.

Portrait and Biographical Record of Arizona. Chicago: Chapman Publishing Co., 1901.

Price, Paxton P. *Mesilla Valley Pioneers, 1823–1912.* Las Cruces, N.M.: Yucca Tree Press, 1995.

Rabaud, Wanda. *The Sainte-Chapelle.* Paris: Éditions Albert Morancé, n.d.

Read, Benjamin M. *An Illustrated History of New Mexico.* Chicago: Lewis Publishing Company, 1895.

Richter, Thomas, ed. "Sister Mallon's Journal." *New Mexico Historical Review* 52, no. 2 (April 1977).

Scobey, Joan M. *Stained Glass: Traditions and Techniques.* New York: The Dial Press, 1979.

Segale, Sister Blandina. *At the End of the Santa Fe Trail.* Columbus, Ohio: Columbian Press, 1932.

Smithsonian Institution. *A Checklist of Keyboard Instruments*. Washington, D.C.:
Smithsonian Institution Press, 1975.

Sonnichsen, C. L. *Tularosa: Last of the Frontier West*. Albuquerque: University of
New Mexico Press, rev. 1980.

Stubbs, Stanley A., and Bruce T. Ellis. *Archaeological Investigations at the Chapel of
San Miguel and the Site of La Castrense*. Laboratory of Anthropology, mono-
graph no. 20. Santa Fe, N.M.: Museum of New Mexico Press, 1955.

Sunder, John E., ed. *Matt Field on the Santa Fe Trail*. Norman: University of
Oklahoma Press, 1960.

Truant, Cynthia Maria. *The Rites of Labor: Brotherhoods of Compagnonnage in Old
and New Regime France*. Ithaca, N.Y.: Cornell University Press, 1994.

Twitchell, Ralph Emerson. *The Leading Facts of New Mexican History*. Vol. 4.
Cedar Rapids, Iowa: Torch Press, 1917.

————. *Old Santa Fe: The Story of New Mexico's Ancient Capital*. Santa Fe, N.M.:
Santa Fe New Mexican Publishing Corporation, 1925.

"Two Members Claim to Have Solved the Riddle of the Miraculous
Stairway." *The Carpenter* (February 1967).

U.S. Bureau of Census.
1870 and 1880, Santa Fe and Socorro Counties, New Mexico.
1880, Titusville, Pennsylvania.

Viollet-le-Duc, Eugène Emmanuel. *Discourses on Architecture*. Trans. by
Benjamin Bucknall. Vol. 1. New York: Grove Press, 1959.

Warner, Louis H. *Archbishop Lamy: An Epoch Maker*. Santa Fe, N.M.: Santa Fe
New Mexican Publishing Corp., 1936.

Webber, F. R. *Church Symbolism*. Cleveland: J. H. Jansen, 1938.

Wolff, Florence, S.L. *From Generation to Generation: The Sisters of Loretto, Their
Constitution and Devotions, 1812–Vatican II*. Louisville, Ky.: General Printing
Company, 1982.

INDEX